Capitalism: A Very Short Introduction

T0055133

VERY SHORT INTRODUCTIONS are for anyone wanting a stimulating and accessible way into a new subject. They are written by experts, and have been translated into more than 45 different languages.

The series began in 1995, and now covers a wide variety of topics in every discipline. The VSI library now contains over 500 volumes—a Very Short Introduction to everything from Psychology and Philosophy of Science to American History and Relativity—and continues to grow in every subject area.

Titles in the series include the following:

ACCOUNTING Christopher Nobes
ADOLESCENCE Peter K. Smith
ADVERTISING Winston Fletcher
AFRICAN AMERICAN RELIGION
    Eddie S. Glaude Jr
AFRICAN HISTORY John Parker and
    Richard Rathbone
AFRICAN RELIGIONS
    Jacob K. Olupona
AGEING Nancy A. Pachana
AGNOSTICISM Robin Le Poidevin
AGRICULTURE Paul Brassley and
    Richard Soffe
ALEXANDER THE GREAT
    Hugh Bowden
ALGEBRA Peter M. Higgins
AMERICAN HISTORY Paul S. Boyer
AMERICAN IMMIGRATION
    David A. Gerber
AMERICAN LEGAL HISTORY
    G. Edward White
AMERICAN POLITICAL
    HISTORY Donald Critchlow
AMERICAN POLITICAL PARTIES
    AND ELECTIONS L. Sandy Maisel
AMERICAN POLITICS
    Richard M. Valelly
THE AMERICAN
    PRESIDENCY Charles O. Jones
THE AMERICAN REVOLUTION
    Robert J. Allison
AMERICAN SLAVERY
    Heather Andrea Williams
THE AMERICAN WEST Stephen Aron

AMERICAN WOMEN'S HISTORY
    Susan Ware
ANAESTHESIA Aidan O'Donnell
ANARCHISM Colin Ward
ANCIENT ASSYRIA Karen Radner
ANCIENT EGYPT Ian Shaw
ANCIENT EGYPTIAN ART AND
    ARCHITECTURE Christina Riggs
ANCIENT GREECE Paul Cartledge
THE ANCIENT NEAR EAST
    Amanda H. Podany
ANCIENT PHILOSOPHY Julia Annas
ANCIENT WARFARE Harry Sidebottom
ANGELS David Albert Jones
ANGLICANISM Mark Chapman
THE ANGLO-SAXON AGE
    John Blair
ANIMAL BEHAVIOUR
    Tristram D. Wyatt
THE ANIMAL KINGDOM
    Peter Holland
ANIMAL RIGHTS David DeGrazia
THE ANTARCTIC Klaus Dodds
ANTISEMITISM Steven Beller
ANXIETY Daniel Freeman and
    Jason Freeman
THE APOCRYPHAL GOSPELS
    Paul Foster
ARCHAEOLOGY Paul Bahn
ARCHITECTURE Andrew Ballantyne
ARISTOCRACY William Doyle
ARISTOTLE Jonathan Barnes
ART HISTORY Dana Arnold
ART THEORY Cynthia Freeland

James Fulcher

CAPITALISM

A Very Short Introduction

SECOND EDITION

OXFORD

UNIVERSITY PRESS

Great Clarendon Street, Oxford, OX2 6DP,
United Kingdom

Oxford University Press is a department of the University of Oxford.
It furthers the University's objective of excellence in research, scholarship,
and education by publishing worldwide. Oxford is a registered trade mark of
Oxford University Press in the UK and in certain other countries

© James Fulcher 2004, 2015

The moral rights of the author have been asserted

First edition published 2004
Second edition published 2015

Impression: 11

Published in the United States of America by Oxford University Press
198 Madison Avenue, New York, NY 10016, United States of America

British Library Cataloguing in Publication Data
Data available

Library of Congress Control Number: 2014958059

ISBN 978–0–19–872607–4

Printed and bound by CPI Group (UK) Ltd, Croydon, CR0 4YY

Contents

List of illustrations

Chapter 1
What is capitalism?

Merchant capitalism

In April 1601 the English East India Company sent its first
expedition to the East Indies. After some eighteen months its
four ships, *Ascension, Dragon, Hector,* and *Susan,* had returned
from Sumatra and Java with a cargo mainly of pepper. The
success of this venture led to a second expedition by the same
ships, which left London in March 1604. On the return journey
Hector and *Susan* set off first, but *Susan* was lost at sea and
Hector was rescued by *Ascension* and *Dragon,* which found her
drifting off South Africa with most of her crew dead. *Ascension,*
Dragon, and *Hector* made it back to England in May 1606 with
a cargo of pepper, cloves, and nutmegs. The shareholders in
these two voyages made a profit of 95 per cent on their
investment.

Despite the similar success of the third expedition in 1607, the
fourth one in 1608, consisting of the ships *Ascension* and *Union,*
was a complete disaster. The *Ascension* reached the west coast of
India but was there wrecked by its 'proud and headstrong master',
who drove his ship aground after ignoring local warnings about
shoaling waters. The *Union* called in at a Madagascan port, where
the crew was ambushed and the captain killed, but nonetheless
the ship made it to Sumatra and loaded a cargo. On her way back,

the *Union* was wrecked off the coast of Brittany. The investors in this expedition lost all their capital.

Capitalism is essentially the investment of money in the expectation of making a profit, and huge profits could be made at some considerable risk by long-distance trading ventures of this kind. Profit was quite simply the result of scarcity and distance. It was made from the huge difference between the price paid for, say, pepper in the Spice Islands and the price it fetched in Europe, a difference that dwarfed the costs of the venture. What mattered was whether the cargo made it back to Europe, though market conditions were also very important, for the sudden return of a large fleet could depress prices. Markets could also become saturated if the high profitability of the trade led too many to enter it. A glut of pepper eventually forced the East India Company to diversify into other spices and other products, such as indigo.

A large amount of capital was needed for this trade. An *East Indiaman,* as the ships engaged in this trade were called, had to be built, fitted out, armed with cannon against Dutch and Portuguese rivals, and repaired, if and when it returned. The Company's shipyards at Blackwall and Deptford, which were major employers of local labour, required financing. Capital was also needed to stock outgoing vessels with bullion and goods to pay for the spices, with munitions, and with food and drink for the large crews they carried. On the Company's third expedition, *Dragon* had a crew of 150, *Hector* 100, and *Consent* 30—in all 280 mouths to feed, at least initially. One reason for the large crews was to make sure there were enough sailors to get the ships back after the hazards of the expedition had taken their toll.

The East India Company's capital was obtained largely but not entirely from the rich London merchants who controlled and administered it. Aristocrats and their hangers-on were another source, and one welcomed by the Company because of their influence at Court. The Company's privileges depended on royal favour. Foreign money was also involved, mainly from Dutch merchants excluded by the rival Dutch East Indies Company. They were also a useful source of intelligence about that company's activities.

The first twelve voyages were each financed separately, with capital committed to one voyage only and the profits of the voyage distributed among its shareholders, according to traditional merchant practices. This was, however, a risky way of financing long-distance trade, for it exposed capital to a long period of uncertainty in far-away and unknown places. Risk could be spread by sending out several ships on each expedition, so that not all the eggs were in one basket, but whole expeditions could, nonetheless, be lost, as in 1608. The company shifted to a method of finance that spread risks over a number of voyages and then became a fully fledged joint-stock company, with, after 1657, continuous investment unrelated to specific voyages. In 1688 trading in its stocks began on the London Stock Exchange.

Risk was also reduced through monopolistic practices. Like its counterparts abroad, the English East India Company was closely intertwined with the state, which granted it a monopoly for the import of oriental goods and gave it the right to export bullion to pay for them. In exchange the state, always short of money, gained revenue from customs duties on the large and valuable imports made by the company. There was certainly competition but it was international competition, in the Indies between the English, the Dutch, and the Portuguese, and as far as possible eliminated within each country. Outsiders were always trying to break into the trade, and one of the key privileges bestowed on the East India Company by the state was the right to take action against 'interlopers'.

Markets were manipulated by buying up stocks and holding back sales. In the 17th century Amsterdam merchants were particularly skilled in these practices and busily established monopolies not only in spices but in Swedish copper, whale products, Italian silks, sugar, perfume ingredients, and saltpetre (an ingredient of gunpowder). Large warehouses were crucial to this and Fernand Braudel comments that the warehouses of the Dutch merchants were bigger and more expensive than large ships. They could hold sufficient grain to feed the entire country for 10–12 years. This was not just a matter of holding goods back to force up prices, for large stocks also enabled the Dutch to destroy foreign competitors by suddenly flooding the whole European market with goods.

This was certainly capitalism, for long-distance trade required a heavy investment of capital in the expectation of large profits, but a free market capitalism it clearly was not. The secret of making high profits was to secure monopolies by one means or another, exclude competitors, and control markets in every way possible. Since profit was made from trading in scarce products rather than rationalizing production, the impact of merchant capitalism on society was limited. Most of the European population could get on with their daily work without being affected by the activities of these owners of capital.

Capitalist production

In the 1780s two Scots, James M'Connel and John Kennedy, travelled south to become apprentices in the Lancashire cotton industry. After gaining experience and making some money in the manufacture of cotton machinery, they set up their own firm in 1795 with an initial capital of £1,770. They soon made good profits from cotton spinning, achieving a return on capital of over 30 per cent in 1799 and 1800. They accumulated capital rapidly and by 1800 their capital had risen to £22,000, by 1810 to £88,000. By 1820 the company had three mills and had established itself as the leading spinner of fine cotton in Manchester, the global metropolis of cotton spinning.

This soon became a very competitive industry, however, and profits could not be sustained at the high level of the early 1800s. This was, indeed, largely because high profits had resulted in expansion and attracted new entrants. There were already 344 cotton mills by 1819 but by 1839 there were 1,815. Technical advances enabled huge increases in productivity during the 1830s, and competition drove companies to invest heavily in the new machinery. The bigger mills built at this time contained 40,000 spindles, as compared with the 4,500 or so of their predecessors. The costs of this heavy investment in buildings and machinery, together with the downward pressure of increased productive capacity on yarn prices, depressed the industry's profitability to low levels in the 1830s.

Profit depended ultimately on the workers who turned raw cotton into yarn (Figure 1). M'Connel and Kennedy's labour force grew from 312 in 1802 to around 1,500 by the 1830s. Much of this was cheap child labour and at times nearly half those employed were

1. Power looms dominate a 19th-century cotton mill.

under the age of 16. In 1819 there were 100 children under the age of 10, some as young as 7, who worked from 6.00 in the morning until 7.30 at night.

Apart from the occasional heavy cost of new factories and new machinery, wages were the company's main cost. Its annual wage bill was over £35,000 by 1811 and over £48,000 by the mid-1830s. Wage costs were minimized not just by holding wage rates down but also by replacing craft workers with less skilled and cheaper labour, as the invention of automatic machinery made this possible. The cyclical instability of the industry resulted in periodic slumps in demand, which forced employers to reduce wages and hours in order to survive.

As industrial capitalism developed, conflict over wages became increasingly organized. The spinners defended themselves against wage reductions through their unions, organizing at first locally but then regionally and nationally. In 1810, 1818, and 1830 there were increasingly organized strikes, but these were defeated by the employers, with the assistance of the state, which arrested strikers and imprisoned union leaders. The employers had created their own associations, so that they could 'black-list' union militants, answer strikes with 'lock-outs', and provide mutual financial support. Vigorous action by the spinners' unions does seem, nonetheless, to have been quite successful, for wages remained stable, in spite of declining profitability and employers' attempts to reduce them.

The exploitation of labour was not just a matter of keeping the wage bill down but also involved the disciplining of the worker. Industrial capitalism required regular and continuous work, if costs were to be minimized. Expensive machinery had to be kept constantly in use. Idleness and drunkenness, even wandering around and conversation, could not be allowed. The cotton mills did indeed have trouble recruiting labour because people simply did not like long, uninterrupted shifts and close supervision.

Employers had to find ways of enforcing a discipline that was quite alien to the first generation of industrial workers. They commonly used the crude and negative sanctions of corporal punishment (for children), fines, or the threat of dismissal, but some developed more sophisticated and moralistic ways of controlling their workers.

Robert Owen introduced 'silent monitors' at his New Lanark mills. Each worker had a piece of wood, with its sides painted black for bad work, blue for indifferent, yellow for good, and white for excellent. The side turned to the front provided a constant reminder, visible to all, of the quality of the previous day's work. Each department had a 'book of character' recording the daily colour for each worker. Discipline was not only a factory matter, for Owen also controlled the community. He sent round street patrols to report drunkenness and fined the drunks next morning. He insisted on cleanliness and established detailed rules for the cleaning of streets and houses. There was even a curfew that required everyone to be indoors after 10.30 p.m. in the winter.

As E. P. Thompson has emphasized, disciplined work was regular, timed work. It meant turning up every day, starting on time, and taking breaks of a specified length at specified times. Employers had a long battle against the well-established tradition of taking off, as additional 'saint's days', 'St Monday', and even 'St Tuesday', to recover from weekend drinking. Time became a battleground, with some unscrupulous employers putting clocks forward in the morning and back at night. There are stories of watches being taken off workers, so that the employer's control of time could not be challenged. Significantly, timepiece ownership spread at the same time as the Industrial Revolution and at the end of the 18th century the government tried to tax the ownership of clocks and watches.

Industrial capitalism not only created work, it also created 'leisure' in the modern sense of the term. This might seem surprising, for the early cotton masters wanted to keep their machinery running as long as possible and forced their employees to work very long hours. However, by requiring continuous work during work hours and ruling out non-work activity, employers had separated out leisure from work. Some did this quite explicitly by creating distinct holiday periods, when factories were shut down, because it was better to do this than have work disrupted by the casual taking of days off. 'Leisure' as a distinct non-work time, whether in the form of the holiday, weekend, or evening, was a result of the disciplined and bounded work time created by capitalist production. Workers then wanted more leisure and leisure time was enlarged by union campaigns, which first started in the cotton industry, and eventually new laws were passed that limited the hours of work and gave workers holiday entitlements.

Leisure was also the creation of capitalism in another sense, through the commercialization of leisure. This no longer meant participation in traditional sports and pastimes. Workers began to pay for leisure activities organized by capitalist enterprises. The new railway companies provided cheap excursion tickets and Lancashire cotton workers could go to Blackpool for the day. In 1841 Thomas Cook organized his first tour, an excursion by rail from Leicester to Loughborough for a temperance meeting. Mass travel to spectator sports, especially football and horse-racing, where people could be charged for entry, was now possible. The importance of this can hardly be exaggerated, for whole new industries were emerging to exploit and develop the leisure market, which was to become a huge source of consumer demand, employment, and profit.

Capitalist production had transformed people's work and leisure lives. The investment of capital in the expectation of profit drove the Industrial Revolution and rapid technical progress increased productivity by leaps and bounds. But machines could not work on their own and it was wage labour that was central to the making of profit. The wage bill was the employer's main cost and became the focus of the conflict between the owners of capital and, as Karl Marx put it, those who owned only their 'labour power', the capacity to make money through physical work. Workers were concentrated in factories and mills, where they had to work in a continuous and disciplined manner under the supervisor's watchful eye, but also now had an opportunity to organize themselves collectively in unions. Non-work activities were expelled from work time into leisure time and daily life was now sharply divided between work and leisure. Wage labour also meant, however, that workers had money to spend on their leisure life. The commercialization of leisure created new industries that fed back into the expansion of capitalist production.

Financial capitalism

On Thursday, 23 February 1995, Nick Leeson, the manager of Baring Securities in Singapore, watched the Nikkei, the Japanese stock market index, drop 330 points. In that one day, Barings lost £143 million through the deals that he had made, though he was the only one who knew what was happening. These losses came on top of the earlier ones of some £470 million that Leeson had kept hidden from his bosses. He knew the game was up and bolted, with his wife, to a hideaway on the north coast of Borneo. Meanwhile Barings' managers, puzzling over the large sums of money that had gone missing in Singapore, tried desperately to find him. By the next morning it was clear that Baring Brothers, the oldest merchant bank in London, had sustained such huge losses that it was effectively bankrupt. Leeson tried to find his way back to England but was arrested in Frankfurt, extradited by Singapore for breaches of its financial regulations, and jailed for six and a half years.

Leeson had been trading in 'derivatives'. These are sophisticated financial instruments that *derive* their value from the value of something else, such as shares, bonds, currencies, or indeed commodities, such as oil or coffee. *Futures,* for example, are contracts to buy shares, bonds, currencies, or commodities at their *current* price at some point in the future. If you think that the price of a share is going to rise, you can buy a three months' future in it. After the three months have expired, you receive shares at the original price and make a profit by selling them at the higher price now prevailing. You can also buy *options,* which do not commit you to the future deal but allow you to decide later whether you want to go ahead or not.

The buying of futures can perform a very important function, since it enables the reduction of uncertainty and therefore risk. If the price of corn is high but the harvest is some way off, a farmer can lock into the existing price by making a deal with a merchant to sell the corn at this price in three months' time. Futures can also, however, be bought for purely speculative reasons to make money out of movements in prices. Financial futures of the kind that Leeson was trading in were more or less informed gambles on future price movements. This was what Susan Strange has called 'casino capitalism'.

Money could also be made from 'arbitrage', which exploits the small price differences that occur for technical reasons between markets. If you are able to spot these differences, calculate rapidly what they are worth, and move large sums of money very quickly, you can make big profits this way. Leeson found that he could exploit small differences, lasting less than a minute, between futures prices on the Osaka and Singapore stock exchanges. Operations of this kind could be carried out with little risk, since an immediate and calculable profit was taken from an existing, if short-lived, price difference.

Why then did things go so wrong for Leeson? He started down a slippery slope when he created a special error account, no. 88888, supposedly to handle innocent dealing and accountancy mistakes.

This was the place where he hid his losses and he also found a way of concealing the accumulated end-of-the-month deficits by getting the Singapore 'back office' to make temporary but illegal transfers of money between various accounts. This and other manipulations bamboozled the auditors, who should have uncovered what was going on.

The existence of 88888 allowed Leeson to gamble with Barings' money. He could build his reputation by taking risks and trading aggressively on the futures markets, since any losses could be hidden. These *could* be covered by later trades and at one time he came close to breaking even, but if he had then closed 88888 down this would have ended the operation that made him the star dealer of Barings. Eventually his losses built up again and accumulated to the point at which they could no longer be concealed just by switching money around.

At this point he plunged into selling options, which, unlike futures, could immediately raise money to cover the monthly shortfalls in 88888. Leeson was gambling heavily on future price movements and the Tokyo stock market went the wrong way. As his losses increased, he raised the stakes by selling more and riskier options, supposedly on behalf of a mythical client called Philippe. When the Nikkei fell after the Kobe earthquake, his losses became so great that he tried single-handedly to force the market up by buying large numbers of futures. The downward pressures were far too strong and the market fell. By now, the losses and liabilities that he had built up were greater than the total capital of Barings.

Why did Barings allow all this to happen? They were a merchant bank which in 1984 had ventured into stockbroking by creating Baring Securities. This was a successful move and by 1989 dealings in mainly Japanese stocks and shares were accounting for half Barings' profits. Baring Securities then moved into the increasingly fashionable activity of derivatives trading. In 1993

Barings merged its capital with that of Barings Securities and in doing so fatally removed the 'fire-wall' protecting the bank from possible losses by its securities department. This was a particularly dangerous thing to do, since senior Barings managers had a poor grasp of the new game that they had entered, while no proper management structure had been put in place and financial controls were very weak. Fraud was an ever-present danger in this financially very complex world and Barings broke a golden rule by allowing Leeson to be both a trader and the manager of the Singapore 'back office', which checked the trades and balanced the books.

Leeson was apparently a very successful dealer who was making large profits for Barings and they backed him to the hilt. Ironically, when Barings crashed, his bosses had just decided to reward his 1994 activities with a £450,000 bonus. As Leeson's operations drained increasing amounts of money from London and sent Barings hunting for loans around the world to cover them, Leeson's bosses actually thought they were financing profitable deals made by their star trader. It was not only the complexities of the financial markets and the extraordinarily weak financial controls within Barings that enabled Leeson to get away with things for so long, but also the corporate hunger for ever greater profits.

What then is capitalism?

We have examined three very different examples of capitalism. The various business activities involved are about as different as they could be, but all involve the investment of money in order to make a profit, the essential feature of capitalism. It is not the nature of the activity itself that matters but the possibility of making profit out of it. Indeed, it is typical of a capitalist society that virtually all economic activities that go on within it are driven by the opportunity to make profit out of capital invested in them.

Capital is money that is invested in order to earn more money. By extension the term capital is often used to refer to money that is *available* for investment or, indeed, any asset that can be readily turned into money for it. Thus, a person's house is often described as their capital, because they can turn it into capital either by selling it or by borrowing on the strength of it. Many small businesses are indeed set up in this way. It is, however, only possible to turn property into capital if its ownership is clearly established, its value can be measured, its title can be transferred, and a market exists for it. A characteristic feature of the development of capitalist societies is the emergence of institutions that enable the conversion of assets of all kinds into capital. Hernando de Soto has argued persuasively that it is the absence of these institutions, above all functioning systems of property law, that frustrates the emergence of local capitalisms in the Third World. He claims that an enormous amount of value that is locked up in property cannot therefore be realized and put by entrepreneurs to productive use.

Capitalists existed before capitalism proper. Since the earliest times merchants have made money by investing in goods that they sold at a profit. As we saw with the East India Company, a merchant capitalism of this kind could be highly organized and very profitable, but it was an activity that involved only a small part of the economy. Most people's livelihoods did not come from economic activities financed by the investment of capital. In capitalism proper the whole economy becomes dependent on the investment of capital and this occurs when it is not just trade that is financed in this way but production as well.

Capitalist production is based on wage labour. A clear line of division and conflict emerges between the owners of capital, who own what Karl Marx called 'the means of production', and those who sell their labour in exchange for wages. The means of production are the workplace, the machinery, and the raw materials, which in pre-capitalist societies were owned not by the owners of capital but by the craftsmen who made the goods. A wage (or salary) is the price paid by the employer for labour sold by the worker. Just as a capitalist will invest money in any activity that brings a profit, a worker can find employment in any activity that pays a wage.

In a capitalist society, both capital and labour have an abstract and disembedded quality, since both are separated from specific economic activities and are therefore able in principle to move into any activity that suitably rewards them. In real life this mobility is constrained by the existing skills and experience of both the owners of capital and workers, and by the relationships and attachments that they have formed. The potential mobility of capital and labour is, nonetheless, one of the features of capitalist societies that gives them their characteristic dynamism.

Wage labour is both free and unfree. Unlike slaves, who are forced to work by their owners, wage labourers can decide whether they work and for whom. Unlike the serfs in feudal society, who were tied to their lord's land, they can move freely and seek work wherever they choose. These freedoms are, on the other hand, somewhat illusory, since in a capitalist society it is difficult to survive without paid work and little choice of work or employer may be available. Wage labourers are also subject to tight control by the employer and, as we saw in the cotton mills, capitalist production meant a new kind of disciplined and continuous work. Workers had become, as Marx put it, 'wage slaves'.

The importance of wage labour is not only its role in production but also its role in consumption. Wage labourers cannot themselves produce what they need or may wish to consume, they have to buy it, thereby providing the demand that activates a whole range of new capitalist enterprises. This applies not only to their food and clothing and personal possessions but to their leisure activities as well. As we saw earlier, capitalist production rapidly led to the creation of whole new industries based on the commercialization of leisure. This double role of wage labour, which enabled the dynamic interaction of production and consumption, explains why capitalist production expanded so very rapidly once it had got going.

Markets, like merchants, are nothing new, but they are central to a capitalist society in a quite new and more abstract way. This is because production and consumption are divorced—people do not consume what they produce or produce what they consume—and are linked only through the markets where goods and services are bought and sold. Instead of being a place where you can buy some extra item that you do not produce yourself, markets become the only means by which you can obtain anything. They are no longer located just in market-places but exist wherever buyers and sellers make their exchanges and, nowadays, this commonly means in some electronic space where prices are listed and deals registered. This applies not only to goods and services but also to labour, money, and capital. The wage, that is the price, for labour is established on a labour market, where employers compete for labour and workers compete for jobs. Money itself is bought and sold on currency markets. The ownership of companies is bought and sold in stock exchanges.

As we saw with the cotton mills, markets generate intense competition between capitalist enterprises. They compete in many different ways by, for example, exploiting labour more efficiently or using technical innovation to reduce costs or marketing products more effectively. Competition forces companies into constant change as they seek to beat the competition or at least keep up with it. Some of course fail and go under, throwing their employees out of work. This competitiveness, which contrasts strongly with the monopolistic practices of merchant capitalism, makes capitalist production exceptionally dynamic.

Capitalist enterprises have, nonetheless, found ways of reducing competition. Those with an edge over their rivals may relish the cut and thrust of competition, but this also creates uncertainty, reduces profits, and causes bankruptcies. Companies thus form trade associations to regulate competition. The market can be rigged by agreeing not to engage in price competition or deciding that all will pay the same wage rates. Competition can also be reduced by mergers and take-overs which concentrate production in fewer hands. There is in capitalism always a tension between competition and concentration, which are equally characteristic of it.

Since prices change, any market provides an opportunity to make money through speculation. This occurs when something is bought in the expectation of selling it at a higher price in the future, without increasing its value by processing it in some way. It can occur in relation to almost any commodity. It may be grain, it may be a currency, it may be a derivative, it may be a slave. Speculation of this kind is often regarded as an unproductive and parasitic activity that is wholly separable from the real economy where goods and services are produced. Unproductive it may often be, but it is not just a means of making money through speculation but also a way of avoiding risk. Since the relationship between supply and demand is always changing, markets are unstable. The building up and storage of stocks is a means of insuring against some adverse price movement that could destroy profit and wipe out a business. Trading in futures, of the kind that Leeson speculated in, is another way of reducing uncertainty and originated long ago as a sophisticated way of protecting producers and traders against unpredictable future movements in prices.

The huge growth in the trading of currency during the 1980s and 1990s followed the shift from fixed to floating exchange rates in the 1970s, which created much greater uncertainty about future currency values. One way of reducing this uncertainty was to 'hedge' one's bets by buying currency futures. So, though the vast bulk of trading in currency futures is undoubtedly speculative, the expansion of this market and the financial innovations associated with it were grounded in real economic needs.

The same argument applies to the speculative trading of company shares. The existence of markets for capital is central to capitalism. They are essential to its functioning since they bring together those seeking to finance economic activities and those with money to invest. Since the stock market prices of companies change, as their economic situation and profitability changes, there are inevitably opportunities for speculating on future price movements. Speculation is not something separate from capitalism but an inevitable outgrowth of its essential machinery.

So, the answer to our question is that capitalism involves the investment of money to make more money. While merchants have long done this, it is when production is financed in this way that a transformative capitalism comes into being. Capitalist production depends on the exploitation of wage labour, which also fuels the consumption of the goods and services produced by capitalist enterprises. Production and consumption are linked by the markets that come to mediate all economic activities. Markets enable competition between enterprises but also generate tendencies towards concentration in order to reduce uncertainty. Market fluctuations also provide the basis of a speculative form of capitalism, which may not be productive but is, nonetheless, based on mechanisms that are central to the operation of a capitalist economy.

Chapter 2
Where did capitalism come from?

Capitalism made its breakthrough in Britain. So it is logical to ask what it was about Britain that provided particularly fertile ground for its growth. Indeed, some accounts of the origins of capitalism content themselves with answering this question. Ellen Meiksins Wood finds its origin in England and, perhaps surprisingly, in agriculture, in the relationships between landlords, tenants, and peasants. The first section of this chapter pursues a similar line of argument that owes much to her approach. But can we stop there? This chapter goes on to argue that capitalism must be seen ultimately as a European phenomenon. In exploring the origins of capitalism, the question is not so much why it developed in Britain but why it emerged in Europe.

Why Britain?

Britain in the 19th century was the first industrial society, but it was the breakthrough of capitalism in the 18th century that made 19th-century industrialism possible. The spread of market relationships and the growth of consumption generated a large enough demand to make investment in industrial production worthwhile. The need to earn money to spend on goods made people seek industrial employment, even though industrial work was monotonous and factory conditions were often grim.

The control of labour by the owners of capital enabled them to increase productivity by concentrating workers in factories, introducing machinery, and organizing labour in new ways.

Relationships between employers and workers in the 18th century already provide clear evidence of capitalist relationships. Trade unions and industrial conflict are generally associated with the 19th century, but organized conflicts of interest between labour and capital were already occurring in the 18th. During this century most craft workers organized themselves at some stage into 'combinations', the forerunners of trade unions. They did this quite simply because collective organization was the only means by which they could protect themselves from the capitalist employers' attempts to cheapen their labour by paying lower wages or employing less-skilled workers.

The wool-combers of the clothing industry in the south-west were one of the first to organize themselves in this way. In 1700 the Tiverton wool-combers formed a 'friendly society', which tried to establish a minimum wage and prevent clothiers employing non-members. They engaged in violent disputes with employers who wanted to import already combed wool from Ireland, an early example of the now familiar strategy of exploiting cheaper labour abroad. The wool-combers responded by burning Irish wool, and attacking the houses of clothiers, attacks on property that resulted in pitched battles with the local constabulary.

It was also in 18th-century Britain that typically capitalist ways of thinking about the economic basis of society were first put forward. The merits of the division of labour, competition, the free operation of the market, and production for profit were clearly laid out by Adam Smith. The key thinkers of this time were examining the mechanisms and principles of the capitalist economy that they saw emerging all around them. Their ideas were then criticized but incorporated, with a rather different ideological spin, in Karl Marx's 19th-century analysis of the dynamics of capitalism.

Why had capitalist production become so extensive in 18th-century Britain? One possible explanation lies in the prior growth of merchant capitalism. As we saw in the first chapter, merchant capitalism, particularly in the shape of the East India Company, grew strongly in the 17th century. Once capital had been accumulated through trade, it could be invested in production. Furthermore, a state-backed merchant capitalism gave rise to an imperial expansion which could provide protected markets for the products of industry. Thus, India was incorporated in the empire during the 18th century and in the 19th the Lancashire cotton industry became largely dependent on the Indian market.

Merchant capitalism was not, however, as closely linked to the growth of capitalist production as these connections would lead one to suppose. It was domestic rather than overseas demand that lay behind the growth of capitalist production in 18th-century Britain. The interdependence of industrial capitalism and empire lay in the future. Anyway, as we saw in Chapter 1, those organizing international trading ventures were not concerned with reducing the costs of production so much as making money out of the huge differences between the prices paid for goods in the East and the prices at which they could be sold in Europe; they were more interested in manipulating markets than developing technology and organizing labour. If they wished to invest their capital in other ways, they were more likely to lend it at a good rate of interest to governments, particularly to rulers seeking to finance their frequent wars.

The origins of capitalist *production* in Britain are to be found less in merchant capitalism than in the earlier growth of production, consumption, and markets in the 16th century. Indeed, the appearance of large enterprises, in, for example, coal mining, has led some to argue that an industrial revolution was already occurring in the 16th century. Although most production at this time was small-scale and carried out on a workshop or household basis, hardly industrial in the modern sense of the word, there was a remarkable growth in the manufacture of clothing and ordinary household goods, such as buttons and ribbons, pins and nails, salt, starch and soap, tobacco pipes, knives and tools, locks, pots and pans, tiles and bricks. Wage labour was becoming increasingly common and over half the households in 16th-century England were at least partly dependent on wage labour. This meant that people had money to buy such goods and market relationships were becoming more important in their daily lives. Distinctively in Britain, a national market based on traders operating out of London had already emerged at this time.

With the growth of wage labour came the first stirrings of class organization. We saw above that in the 18th century craft workers were becoming extensively organized in 'combinations'. The very beginnings of worker organization can, however, be found considerably before this. 'Journeymen's societies' were well established in 16th-century Britain and can be traced back to the 14th. Journeymen, literally 'day-workers', were employed by a master for a short period of time. They varied in skill but were commonly craftsmen who had completed an apprenticeship but not yet acquired sufficient skill and experience to qualify as a master. Increasingly masters tried to keep them as cheap labour by obstructing their qualification as masters and excluding them from the guild organizations that controlled the crafts. The journeymen's response was organization, to defend their status and bargain collectively for improvements in wages and working conditions. Although there was still much that was medieval in the ritual activities of their associations, they also used quite modern weapons. In Coventry in 1424 the journeymen in the clothing trade went on strike for higher wages and the town authorities had to intervene to bring about a settlement. Thus, at this early time, craftsmen were already becoming divided into an employing and a labouring class that were in conflict with each other.

Little capital was at this stage involved in most craft production, but in some trades, notably clothing, a new form of production, the 'putting-out system', was coming into existence. In the case of clothing, merchants used their capital to buy wool and put this out to spinners and weavers, before collecting the cloth, distributing it to other crafts for finishing off, and finally selling it. Although this system was organized by merchants, they were much closer than those engaged in international trading ventures to the production process. They were, indeed, commonly craftsmen by origin.

This was a clear and important step on the road to capitalist production. It was not capitalist production proper, for the owner of the capital owned the raw material and the product but did not own the whole of the means of production. Weavers, for example, generally worked at home on their own looms. Production was dispersed through many small units and the merchant did not control the production process or directly supervise the worker. However, in later forms of this system weavers might rent their looms from their capitalist employer, or rent workplaces in workshops owned by the employer, who thereby acquired greater control over them. The putting-out system shaded into the modern factory, though it also persisted alongside it and in the textiles industry still does, for in this industry finishing-off work is still commonly put out to home workers.

Thus, we can trace the origins of capitalist production a long way back, to the 16th century and earlier. What was it about British society that accounts for these early tendencies towards capitalism? Arguably, it was changes in the social relationships of the countryside.

Feudal lords had lived off their rights to receive produce, labour, or money payments from an unfree peasantry that was tied to the land, but in the 15th-century market relationships were beginning to supersede feudal ones. Lords were becoming landowners, who lived off the rent paid by tenant farmers, who competed in a market for these tenancies. The land was worked increasingly by wage labour and was also becoming property that could be bought and sold.

The enclosure movement, which began in the late 15th century and continued intermittently into the 19th, symbolizes these changes in landownership. This movement fenced off land, sometimes turning what had been common land available to all into private property, and forcing off the land local people who had relied on their right to exploit common land (Figure 2). Sometimes enclosure simply reorganized the traditionally

2. The landscape of enclosure: the mid-18th-century estate of David Wells at Burbage in Leicestershire, showing a model farm surrounded by enclosed fields.

scattered parcels of land held by particular individuals into single, more easily managed, units. The outcome was the division of land into distinct blocks owned by particular individuals. Thus, enclosure cut through complex medieval patterns of land usage and turned land into marketable property.

A market-oriented agriculture contributed to the development of capitalist production in crucial ways. Competition between farmers resulted in innovation and a greater productivity that enabled them to provide food for a growing non-agricultural population. The farmers who marketed their produce, and their waged agricultural workers, had money to spend on consumer goods. Greater agricultural efficiency released labour for employment in making these goods, which were, indeed, produced increasingly in the rural areas where new centres of production were emerging.

Why did market relationships replace feudal ones? One commonly argued reason for the decline of feudal relationships was the impact of the Black Death. In 15th-century England the feudal lords' ability to enforce their rights and control the movement of a subject peasantry had collapsed, largely as a consequence of this disease. The Black Death had reduced the population by around a third in the mid-14th century and empowered a now much smaller agricultural labour force to resist lords' attempts to enforce their rights. Since labour was scarce, peasants could flee oppressive lords and find employment elsewhere. The Black Death was, however, a European phenomenon, which did not have the same consequences everywhere, and cannot itself explain the earlier decline of feudalism in Britain.

So, why did feudalism decline earlier in Britain? Arguably, because it had been less solidly established here. In truly feudal societies judicial and military authority were dispersed to local lords. They used the power that this decentralization of right and might gave them to subordinate and exploit the peasantry. According to Ellen Meiksins Wood, England had, however, been a relatively unified, orderly, and cohesive monarchy since the Norman conquest in 1066. By the 16th century, under the Tudors, it had become the least feudal, the most unified and centralized of European states. The English ruling class made less use of local military power to extract a surplus from the peasantry than its continental counterparts did. It relied more on the economic mechanisms provided by landownership, rent, and wage labour. A relatively unified state also facilitated the emergence of a national market.

So, in seeking an answer to the question—Why was Britain the first capitalist society?—we end up in 1066. But this is not to suggest that the arrow in the eye of King Harold caused capitalism to develop in Britain! It is rather that the consequences of the Norman conquest eventually produced a society more favourable than other European societies were to the emergence of a fully fledged capitalism.

Capitalism in Europe

Although Britain was the first society in which production in general became capitalist, there are plentiful examples of the emergence of capitalism elsewhere in Europe. Indeed, the techniques of capitalist organization were at times much more advanced in other European societies.

Capitalist production already had a long history in Europe. The putting-out system seems to have originated in either Flanders or Italy, and had become widespread in 14th- and 15th-century Germany. In Flanders it was initially organized by master weaver-drapers who required little capital for their operations, but by the 13th century the growth there of a luxury cloth trade, with a more complex production process, led to the emergence of 'merchant-entrepreneurs' employing large amounts of capital.

This industry imported English wool. The commercialization of agriculture in England was therefore linked to capitalist cloth production in Flanders, clear proof of the need to treat capitalism as European in character.

Merchant capital also became heavily involved in continental mining operations. At the end of the 15th century, merchant capitalists reorganized mining in northern and central Europe. After deposits close to the surface had been exhausted, deep mining, whether of copper, gold, silver, or lead, required large amounts of capital and this provided an opportunity for merchants, such as the Fuggers of Augsburg, to move in and take control of production. The Fuggers had made their fortune from trade and loans to the Hapsburg emperors but then increased it further by investing in mining operations in Austria and Hungary. Their Hungarian mine employed hundreds of workers and was highly profitable. It was in the mines of central Europe that the previously independent miners became wage labour, and the word *arbeiter*, German for worker, first came into use at this time.

There were also early signs of a movement towards capitalist production in some continental cities. This was particularly evident in the rapidly developing printing industry. Even though most printing works were small, capital was required to buy the presses and pay for wages, paper, and type. Profits depended on keeping the cost of labour down and there were frequent conflicts between print-masters and their workers, who became highly organized in journeymen's associations. There was a big printers' strike in Lyons in 1539, which spread to Paris in 1541, and there were further flare-ups in these cities in 1567 and 1571.

Capitalist production was then developing all over Europe, not only in Britain, but the growth of capitalism should not be seen just from the perspective of production. The early development of the commercial and financial techniques of capitalism occurred outside Britain. Merchant capitalism was more developed in

17th-century Holland than 17th-century Britain, and key innovations in company finance were made by the Dutch East India Company, well before they were adopted by its British counterpart. The Dutch company's capital was made permanent in 1609. Investors now received dividends from a 'joint-stock' company and could no longer withdraw their capital, though they could sell their shares. This innovation gave companies a more permanent and independent existence by enabling them to build up their capital on a long-term basis. It also created a market in shares and it was no accident that a stock exchange was established in Amsterdam at the same time (Figure 3).

As we saw in the first section of this chapter, these innovations in merchant capitalism probably had little to do with the growth of capitalist production. The world of the East Indies companies and associated stock markets had little connection with manufacturing. Indeed, the early stages of industrialization in Britain were not financed by investment through joint-stock companies, as the

3. The Amsterdam stock exchange, built 1608–13.

account in Chapter 1 of the rise of M'Connel and Kennedy shows. Most early industrial enterprises were relatively small operations that were funded by families or local loans and then accumulated capital from their profits.

Financial innovations were, however, critical to the growth of the large industrial corporations that in the later 19th century came to dominate capitalist production. If we are to understand the origins of the capitalist world that we live in, an understanding of the growth of large corporations is arguably as important as an understanding of the emergence of capitalist production itself. The great break with the past was not so much the rise of capitalist production, which emerged very gradually through a series of small steps, but the establishment of large, capital-intensive operations organized by great corporations. From this perspective, the financial innovations of merchant capitalism in 17th-century Holland were of immense importance.

These innovations can themselves be traced back from 17th-century Holland to 16th-century Antwerp. There, merchants had developed new ways of financing their trading ventures and spreading risk by drawing on the capital of a wider circle of 'passive' investors. Antwerp was also the centre of a financial revolution based on bills of exchange. These had long existed as a crucial lubricant of trade, for they enabled merchants to pay locally for goods they had bought somewhere else, maybe on the other side of Europe. In the 16th century they were no longer tied to particular trading transactions but became a means of moving money around internationally, thereby enabling the creation of a European capital market. There were also the beginnings of futures trading with the establishment in Antwerp of a commodities market called the 'English House', where contracts to buy English wool were traded without wool ever changing hands.

And we can go back further, for the forerunners of these methods of raising capital and financing trade can be found in the Italian cities, notably Genoa and Venice, of the 12th century. The earliest form of bills of exchange originated in late 12th-century Genoa. The risks of international trade led merchants in the cities to develop new forms of partnership to finance voyages and share risks and profits. By the 14th century advances in book-keeping enabled a much closer control of international trading operations. Innovations of this kind, which figured prominently in early accounts of the history of capitalism, have been sidelined by the more recent emphasis on the development of capitalist production. An understanding of the origins of the corporate and financial capitalism that dominate the contemporary world requires that we put them back in.

These innovations could spread rapidly from the financially and commercially most advanced centres in first Italy, then Flanders, then Holland through the trading and financial networks that criss-crossed Europe, for medieval business was European in its scope. The leading Italian merchant and banking houses had branches in Flanders, England, and France in the 14th century. They even financed the overseas military adventures of the kings of England.

It was also not just business relationships that created such networks but the movement of refugees, particularly in the 16th and 17th centuries. In the second half of the 16th century refugees from Italy and Flanders carried their knowledge, skills, and capital to other countries, to Switzerland, Germany, Holland, and England. The Huguenots, French Protestants with Calvinist beliefs, migrated or were expelled to England and Switzerland and there started new industries, such as lace-making, silk manufacture, and watch-making. Jewish merchants were expelled from Iberia and dispersed all over Europe, some moving to Antwerp and, after their expulsion from there, to Amsterdam.

Its openness to refugees contributed significantly to the development of capitalist production in England. In a discussion of England's economic rise that resonates interestingly with today's debate on immigration, Carlo Cipolla has argued that the economic contribution of refugees has been neglected and comments on the 'extraordinary cultural receptiveness' of Elizabethan England. Indeed, deliberate efforts were made at this time to revive declining clothing industries by bringing in from France and Flanders refugee craftsmen familiar with the latest techniques and products. It was not only the textiles industry that benefited, for new techniques in glass-making, paper-making, and iron-working were also brought in by refugees.

Refugee movements were generated by the religious intolerance and wars of religion that followed the Reformation and Counter-Reformation, though it was not only for religious reasons that people migrated. The economic disruption caused by warfare and military occupation was another major reason for the exodus from Flanders to Holland. It is also not easy to distinguish economic refugees from refugees of conscience and belief, as in today's world. The areas the refugees left were broadly speaking those that were economically stagnant or in decline and those where they settled were in the forefront of economic development. Economic leadership shifted from Italy to Germany and Flanders, then to Holland, and only later to Britain. Although, as we have seen, both consumption and production had been growing steadily in Britain for centuries, it was not until the 18th century that Britain overtook Holland to become the leading capitalist country in Europe.

Changes in economic leadership could result from shifts in trade, the impact of war, or political and religious change, but they were, as in our own day, partly the result of international competition and the self-undermining consequences of success. Thus, Italian economic decline in the 16th century resulted partly from the shift of trade from the Mediterranean to the Atlantic but was also the result of competition from lower-cost producers in northern Europe. The Italian cities had provided an environment in which crafts producing high-quality goods could flourish, but wages had risen, while the guilds and their regulations prevented innovation. Local attempts to stamp out lower-cost production in rural areas only made the situation worse. The less developed countries of northern Europe, like some less developed Third World countries today, could out-compete the established centres of production.

Thus, while one may reasonably ask why Britain was the first country in which production became capitalist, it is quite wrong to seek the origins of capitalism solely in Britain. This is partly because crucial features of capitalist organization originated outside Britain. It is above all, however, because distinct national capitalisms did not exist at the time when capitalism was emerging. Business networks were European, merchants and workers moved around between countries, and different parts of Europe led the development of capitalism at different times.

Why Europe?

What was it that made Europe the birth-place of capitalism? Virtually every distinctive feature of European society has been advanced by someone as *the* explanation of the emergence of capitalism in Europe.

One possible answer lies in Europe's cities. There has already been much reference in this chapter to the role of cities in the development of capitalism. The Italian cities, then Bruges, Antwerp, Amsterdam, and London, were the source of key innovations in financial and commercial techniques. One of the distinctive features of European society was the emergence in Italy, Flanders, and Germany of networks of relatively independent city-states where commercial and financial, rather than landed, interests ruled.

Cities played an indispensable role, but there are problems with making them *the* explanation of the emergence of capitalism in Europe. There was certainly a period between the 11th and 13th centuries when cities became increasingly independent, but in the centuries that followed they lost much of their autonomy, first to resurgent feudal rulers and then to the nation-state. Also, capitalist production developed more strongly in the countryside than the city, for the guilds in the cities obstructed the ruthless capitalist pursuit of new methods and cheaper labour. Furthermore, as argued in the first part of this chapter, in Britain, at least, changes in agriculture were crucial to the growth of capitalist production.

Perhaps the answer lies in feudalism itself. The relationship between feudalism and capitalism is intriguing and paradoxical. In many ways feudalism appears quite opposite in character to capitalism. Under feudalism, power and wealth were linked to the control of land not the ownership of capital. Production was not for the market but for consumption by the producer and the lord, who used physical rather than economic coercion to extract the surplus from the producer. There was no 'free' wage labour, for agricultural labour was tied to the land. How could such a society give rise to capitalism?

Although feudal societies have been viewed as reservoirs of anti-capitalist conservatism, they were in many ways flexible and dynamic. Such key features of capitalism as markets and wage labour could emerge within feudal society, and more easily than in either slave-based societies, such as ancient Rome, or the self-sufficient peasantries found in much of the rest of the world. Under feudalism producers had, on the one hand, some degree of freedom, because, unlike slaves, they had limited and specified obligations to their lord. On the other hand, unlike independent and self-sufficient peasants, they were forced to produce a surplus.

A transition to a market economy could also be made relatively easily. Peasants' obligations to provide labour services or produce for the lord could be replaced by money payments, which in turn meant that peasants had to earn money through wage labour or the sale of produce in markets. Lords themselves stimulated trade and manufacturing by spending their ill-gotten gains on luxury products. The class conflict inherent in feudalism could also contribute to this transition, for lords were constantly devising new ways of extracting money from the peasantry, who fought back by exploiting labour shortages to free themselves from feudal obligations and obtain wages in exchange for their labour.

One must add that feudalism did not inevitably shift into capitalism in this way. It did so in Western Europe but not in Eastern Europe, where landowners actually increased the feudal exploitation of the peasantry in the 16th century, in order to make more money from the export of grain to the cities of Western Europe. Thus, the economic development of Western Europe for a time at least intensified feudalism elsewhere. Feudalism had the *potential* to evolve into capitalism but whether it did so or not depended on other factors. In a well-known contribution to the debate on this question, Robert Brenner has argued that the peasants' capacity to organize against their feudal lords and free themselves from feudal bonds was here critical. In the West, lords had less control of villages than they had in the East.

Another approach starts from the multi-state political structure of Europe. After the collapse of Rome no ruler was able to establish imperial control over the whole of Europe, though many tried. Some have explained this failure by reference to the ethnic diversity stemming from the multiple barbarian invasions that destroyed Rome. The inability to construct successor empires resulted also from the feudal structure of medieval monarchies. The military and financial weakness of feudal rulers, who were dependent on the military service of unreliable followers and unable to mobilize sufficient resources, doomed their imperial ventures to failure.

But why was the multi-state structure so conducive to the rise of capitalism? The argument here is in part a negative one, for it is claimed that imperial bureaucracies inhibit capitalist dynamism through their taxes, their regulations, and their general subordination of economic development to political stability. There is also the positive point that Europe did not fall into anarchy, for kingdoms were constructed that provided the minimal degree of order necessary for economic development.

The multi-state character of Europe also made it possible for entrepreneurs to move from countries where the economic environment was deteriorating to those providing more favourable conditions for enterprise. Thus, the stifling effects of the rise of the Counter-Reformation state in Italy and Flanders did not halt the development of capitalism, because people could move to places where the political regime was less bureaucratic and more tolerant.

As we saw earlier, one of the striking features of the development of capitalism in Europe was the periodic movement of its leading edge from one country to another. As conditions deteriorated in one area, entrepreneurs could find pastures new somewhere else.

Perhaps, however, it was distinctive ideas rather than distinctive structures that resulted in the development of capitalism in Europe. Religious beliefs motivate people, give their actions meaning, and regulate their behaviour through norms that specify how they should live. There is certainly no doubt that powerful religious institutions penetrated into every corner of people's lives in medieval Europe. Were there connections between Christianity and the development of capitalism?

The best-known connection is that made by Max Weber between the 'Protestant ethic' and the 'spirit of capitalism'. Weber was not, it should be noted, arguing that Protestantism caused capitalism but rather that it provided a set of ideas that motivated people to behave in capitalist ways. Protestant beliefs, especially those of the Calvinists (or Puritans, as they were called in Britain), drove people to lead an abstemious life, to save rather than spend, and therefore resulted in the accumulation of capital. Protestants also believed that God should be served not by a religious withdrawal from life but through the proper conduct of the occupation that God had called them to perform. Protestantism brought the religious discipline of the monastery into everyday economic activity and Weber quotes a 16th-century Protestant theologian declaring that 'you think you have escaped from the monastery, but everyone must now be a monk throughout his life'.

This puritan work ethic certainly left its imprint on the attitudes towards work and money typically found in the capitalist societies of northern Europe and North America but, as an explanation of the emergence of capitalism, it has been found wanting. Plentiful examples of Calvinist entrepreneurs can certainly be found, and there was greater economic growth in countries where Calvinism had taken root, but there is not enough evidence that it was Calvinist *beliefs* that were crucial to the emergence of capitalism. Indeed, Henry Kamen has convincingly argued that it was not the religious beliefs of Protestant entrepreneurs but their refugee status that accounted for the apparent relationship between Calvinism and capitalism.

Similarly, Trevor-Roper argued that the Counter-Reformation state drove entrepreneurs out of Catholic areas, notably Italy and Flanders, which had previously been the leading economic centres, into the Calvinist countries of northern Europe. This was partly due to a new religious intolerance, which forced out not only Protestants but also Jews and non-fanatical Catholics with broadly humanistic beliefs, of the kind typically held by Catholic entrepreneurs. It was also because the bureaucracy and high taxation of the Counter-Reformation state were inimical to entrepreneurial activity. Some of the refugees were Calvinist by belief but others became Calvinist by convenience because they ended up in areas where Calvinism was the local religion.

The other side to the debate around the religious origins of capitalism in Europe is the claim that the religions of other civilizations inhibited the emergence of capitalism there. Confucianist China provides an interesting case in point. Its advanced civilization was able to produce many important innovations, inventing paper and gunpowder, but these did not become the basis of an industrial capitalism. Confucianist beliefs in the orderliness of both the natural and social worlds arguably encouraged social stability rather than the dynamism characteristic of capitalism. Michio Morishima has, however, argued that it was the Japanese variant of Confucianism that was largely responsible for the development of a successful state-organized capitalism in Japan.

China was also the opposite of Europe in other respects. It was a bureaucratic empire that lacked the feudal decentralization, autonomous cities, and multi-state competitiveness characteristic of Europe. We cannot therefore isolate the effect of religious differences from other differences that plausibly account for the emergence of capitalism in Europe rather than China.

Rather than expecting that other advanced civilizations would generate capitalism, there are, in any case, good reasons why they did not. Most advanced civilizations were dominated by a single ruling group that used military or religious, rather than economic, coercion to scoop off the surplus from those who produced crops and goods. This surplus was then used for territorial expansion, the maintenance of military power, and projects and displays that enhanced prestige. Some form of bureaucratic apparatus was constructed to tax, regulate, and subordinate the population. Individuals certainly accumulated exceptional wealth and possessions in these societies, but through their connections with the state rather than purely economic activity. There were, in other words, easier ways to become rich and powerful than through the accumulation of capital and the management of labour.

The absence in Europe of a single, cohesive, and totally dominant elite of this kind is the common factor that brings together the various explanations we have been considering. Post-Roman Europe was characterized by political fragmentation, dynastic competition, urban autonomy, and a continual struggle between rulers and ruled. Money could certainly be made through connections with rulers, but states were unstable, rulers were unreliable, and coercion was met with resistance. In these circumstances economic activity could become a more attractive means of acquiring, increasing, and maintaining wealth.

The economic mechanisms of market transactions, capital accumulation, and wage labour gradually replaced bureaucratic and feudal means of building it up. The unique structural features of European society provided the conditions in which the machinery of capitalism could emerge and flourish.

Chapter 3
How did we get here?

Capitalism transformed the world but has itself been transformed. We are now in a quite distinct era in its development, one that began in the latest transformation during the 1970s and 1980s. To understand where we are now, we do need, however, to set this new era in historical context. Thatcherism, which embodied its central ideas, set out to reverse many of the tendencies of the previous hundred years and restore the values and vigour of capitalism in the Victorian age.

This chapter examines the development of industrial capitalism by dividing it into three stages. These stages and the labels given to them should not be taken too seriously. They are simply a convenient way of bringing out the distinctive character of different periods and the interconnections between their main features. The stages are outlined with reference to British history, for Britain produced the first industrial capitalism and has been the main source of the key ideas and institutions of capitalist society. Chapter 4 considers international differences in the development of capitalism.

Anarchic capitalism

This was the stage in the 18th and early 19th centuries when industrial capitalism made its breakthrough. It was anarchic because the activities of capitalist entrepreneurs were relatively unchecked either by organized labour or the state. Small factories and workshops engaged in intense competition with each other, while labour was mobile, pouring into and building the new industrial cities, and constructing the canals, roads, and railways that made possible the mass transportation of goods and people.

As Chapter 2 showed, craftsmen had been trying to organize themselves into associations that would give them some collective power since the earliest days of capitalist production. Employer hostility, intensified by competitive pressures, together with unstable employment and the small size of most units of production, made it very hard for workers to organize but did not stop them trying. In the early 19th century there were numerous and increasingly ambitious attempts to form general unions of all workers. In 1830 the National Association for the Protection of Labour was founded and in 1834 the Grand National Consolidated Union, though neither lasted long. At this time the only unions that could survive were those of skilled workers, who were able to control entry to their craft and were not easily replaceable.

The state did begin to regulate the conditions of factory work. Attempts to limit the number of hours that children could work had their first success in the Health and Morals of Apprentices Act of 1802, though it was not until the 1833 Factory Act that the first effective legislation to do this was passed. The frequently told story of increasing factory regulation gives, however, a somewhat misleading picture of the state's involvement in the economy at this time, for important aspects of economic life were being deregulated.

The state machinery set up in the 16th century to regulate apprenticeships, wage-rates, and food prices was abolished by 1815. The freeing of international trade took longer but was achieved by the 1860s. The key step in this was the ending of import duties on corn in 1846. Deregulation was in the interests of industrialists, who wanted the freedom to develop their activities without state interference. They wanted wage-rates to be set by the labour market not by the state. They also wanted free trade, in part to assist exports but also because imports of cheap food would allow them to pay lower wages.

Deregulation was in tune with the rise at this time of liberal beliefs in the freedom of the individual and the free operation of the market but did not mean that the state totally withdrew. In fact, the very reverse was the case, for market forces could operate freely only within an orderly society, which required a strengthening of the state at a time when industrial capitalism was generating great disorder. Strikes, rioting, machine-breaking, and crimes against property were threatening both production and order, while trade unions and radical political movements directly challenged the capitalist employer and the state. The military were deployed to quell riots and demonstrations, sometimes with considerable violence.

State welfare hardly existed at this time. The rising number of poor people without means of support did become a cause of increasing concern. This was not because of a concern for their welfare but rather because of a fear that they would become a burden on the local community. They had to be forced to work, and in 1834 the Poor Law Amendment Act introduced a new system of relief to do just that. The existing practice of outdoor relief was abolished and a system of indoor relief created. Only those who entered a 'workhouse' would be given support. Conditions there would be made worse than those experienced by the poorest paid worker, so that only those unable to work would enter. This law generated enormous hostility amongst the poor, and in practice the old system of outdoor relief largely continued, but the 1834 law illustrates well the attitude of the state to poverty during the period of anarchic capitalism.

Competitive small-scale manufacturing, weak labour organization, economic deregulation, a strong state, and minimal state welfare were the mutually reinforcing features of this stage in the development of capitalism. Liberal beliefs in the freedom of the individual were particularly characteristic of this period but not just of historical significance. Liberalism persisted as a powerful set of ideas, which later resurfaced in the 'neo-liberal' guise of the beliefs and policies that have been so influential during the most recent stage of capitalist development.

Managed capitalism

During the next stage in the development of capitalism, which began in the second half of the 19th century and came to its peak in the 1970s, competition and regulation by the market declined as both sides of industry became more organized and as state management and control increased. International conflict also played its part in this, as governments both sought to protect national economies from a growing international competition and more effectively manage and mobilize their resources against their enemies.

Class organization was one of the main driving forces behind the developments of this next stage. More stable economic growth after the middle of the 19th century, the emergence of larger units of production (Figure 4), and the construction of stronger union organizations produced the conditions in which a national labour movement could at last emerge and survive. Employers too became more organized. Employers' associations were establishing themselves in the second half of the 19th century, as employers banded together at industry level, partly in order to counter the growing industrial power of the unions but also to reduce the uncertainties generated by unregulated competition.

The main way in which employers reduced uncertainty was not, however, through association but through concentration. The

4. The Cyclops steelworks in Sheffield, 1853: large units concentrated production and facilitated the organization of labour.

simplest way of dealing with the competition was to buy it up or merge with it. In Britain this process got strongly under way towards the end of the 19th century and there was a further wave of mergers in the 1920s. This notably resulted in the 1926 creation of ICI (Imperial Chemical Industries) out of four chemical companies that were themselves the products of earlier mergers. Increasing concentration has always been one of the main tendencies in capitalist organization and shows little sign of ceasing.

As corporate units became larger, the management function grew and with it managerial occupations and associations. Some now claimed that a 'managerial revolution' was changing the character of capitalist industrialism. They argued that the growth of management, together with the spread of share ownership to many small and powerless owners, meant that managers rather than shareholders now controlled corporations. Instead of seeking simply to maximize profits, managers took account of the interests of all with a stake in the company. Plausible as it was, this notion of a 'managerial revolution' overstated the power of managers, for owners were still ultimately in control and profitability remained the 'bottom line', but industrial production was undoubtedly a much more managed process than it had been before. Indeed, Alfred Chandler has argued convincingly that the 20th-century supremacy of the American corporation was due to the 'organizational capabilities' of American management. This was one sense in which capitalism had become increasingly 'managed'.

In Britain, it also became more managed in other ways, as governments responded to class organization by becoming more involved in the management of class relationships. The state shifted from the repression of working class discontent to its management through incorporation, that is through the inclusion and representation of the working class. In the political arena, incorporation took the form of extending the right to vote, most notably in 1867, and the subsequent competition for working class votes between the existing political parties, which delayed the emergence of the Labour Party into the 20th century. This was not founded until 1906, long after comparable parties had been established in other European countries. In the industrial arena, the unions were given some legislative protection during the 1870s, though the employers still took occasional action against them through the courts, until the Trade Disputes Act of 1906 provided them with immunity from civil actions.

The British state also increasingly took responsibility for people's welfare. This process began with public health measures in the mid-19th century, but it was not until the decade before the First World War that the foundations of the modern welfare state were laid with the provision of state pensions, of unemployment, disability, and maternity benefits, and of sick pay and free medical treatment by general practitioners. In the 1940s the construction of the welfare state was completed with the provision of free secondary education, the founding of the National Health Service, and the extension of benefits to provide a universal safety-net. Employment is crucial to welfare and the experience of the 1930s depression made the maintenance of 'full employment' one of the highest priorities of postwar governments.

Not only were education and health taken out of the market-place but also other important industries and services. This process started locally with the so-called 'municipal socialism' of the last quarter of the 19th century, which took gas and water supply into public ownership and provided publicly owned city transport. The public provision of housing began with the 1890 law that gave councils the power to build houses. The taking of telephone companies into public ownership began in 1892. Then in the 20th century electricity generation, broadcasting, civil aviation, the railways, coal mining, and many other industries too numerous to list here were created or taken over by the state. Much of this 'nationalization' was motivated not by socialist beliefs in the merits of public ownership but by nationalist concerns with the public ownership of key services and the inefficiency of fragmented or backward industries.

The political incorporation of the working class, the rise of the Labour Party, and socialist ideas evidently played an important part in all this, but it was also driven by international conflict. The breakthrough in the development of state welfare came during the decade before the First World War when there were concerns with the poor physical condition of British soldiers during the Boer War and an awareness of the superior development of state welfare in imperial Germany. The First World War then led to a huge extension of state control over the economy and, although much of this was dismantled afterwards, it did establish important precedents for the future expansion of state ownership. The First World War also boosted class organization, with both the unions and the employers developing more centralized national organizations, in order to influence a government becoming heavily involved in economic management.

The rivalries between empires which lay behind much of the international conflict of the first half of the 20th century drove forward many of the features of managed capitalism, but this was not the only relationship between empires and managed capitalism. As international competition increased after industrial capitalism spread from Britain to other countries, free trade was eventually displaced by a protectionism that reached its peak in the 1930s. Markets could be protected, and the supply of cheap raw materials maintained, by fencing off one's empire from competitor nations. This protection also made it possible for employers to arrive at compromises with the unions that could not have been sustained in the face of increasing competition from countries with higher productivity or lower wages.

In the quarter century or so after the Second World War managed capitalism reached its fullest extent. It was in the 1940s that a welfare state was fully established and the last big burst of nationalization occurred, though some ailing companies were still being taken into public ownership in the 1970s. Public sector housing expanded and at its peak in 1979 a remarkable third of British households were in the public sector. The governments of the 1960s and 1970s tried to regulate prices and incomes through deals with the unions and employers that offered them some influence over government policy in exchange for cooperation in its implementation. Governments also tried to pursue countercyclical policies that would maintain employment levels. Equality issues were politically prominent, particularly in relation to education, taxation, and welfare.

The evident deficiencies and intense conflicts of anarchic capitalism had generated the contrasting organizations, institutions, and ideologies of a 'managed capitalism', which had a distinctive and coherent character. This second stage was shaped by the growth of large corporations, the development of class organization, corporatist relationships between the state and class organizations, state intervention and regulation, state welfare, and the extension of public ownership, which were interrelated and mutually reinforcing processes. What they all had in common was a reduction in the significance of market relationships in people's lives, reflecting a general reaction against the dehumanizing impact of the market forces that had increasingly shaped the way that people lived during capitalism's breakthrough period. The dynamics of capitalism alone cannot, none the less, account for the development of managed capitalism. It was the national and international context that allowed and assisted these processes to develop, for during this stage capitalism was organized within national empires.

Remarketized capitalism

In the 1960s the welfare state, corporatist relationships between governments and major interest organizations, and extensive public ownership all appeared to be well-established features of British society. The structures and values of managed capitalism had been evolving for at least a century and it looked as though they would continue to develop into the foreseeable future. They certainly had their critics, on the Right and the Left, but were not seriously questioned by mainstream politicians until the end of the 1960s. Yet, during the 1970s managed capitalism collapsed and in the 1980s a new orthodoxy, centred on the revival of market forces, imprinted itself on government policy.

Why did managed capitalism collapse? One reason for this was that its corporatist institutions could not in the end be made to work. Government attempts to regulate prices and incomes failed time after time, because the cooperation they required between unions, employers, and the state was either not forthcoming or could not be engineered. When governments adopted more coercive policies, they met a union resistance they could not overcome, a resistance that could prove fatal to the governments themselves. In 1974 the Conservative government's inability to deal with a miners' strike against its incomes policy resulted in electoral defeat, and Labour lost the 1979 election after a 'winter of discontent', when its incomes policy fell apart in a wave of public sector strikes.

It was argued at the time that this failure to make managed capitalism work was a result of the peculiar organizational deficiencies of British industrial relations. This was plausible, given the decentralized and archaic organization of both unions and employers. Their structures had been shaped in the 19th century and had not adapted to economic and social change. Furthermore, corporatist institutions appeared to work smoothly in Sweden, with its more centralized, symmetrical, and functional structures. But Swedish institutions too went into disarray in the 1970s, as the next chapter will show. There was more to the problems of managed capitalism than the archaic character of British institutions.

The real problem was that increasing international competition was putting the old industrial societies under growing pressure. With the decline of empires, and the growth of free trade, national insulation was breaking down. The economies of the recently defeated but highly productive nations, West Germany and Japan, were reviving. Employers responded to increasing competition by trying to reduce labour costs, which meant holding down wages, or shedding workers, or increasing productivity, all of which were unpopular with workers and resisted by their unions. As managed capitalism had developed, these unions had increased both their membership and their power so that they were in a strong position to resist changes they saw as against their members' interests.

There were also broader changes in values and priorities, which signalled a popular reaction against managed capitalism. There was a growing revolt against higher taxation and a rising dissatisfaction with the take-it-or-leave-it attitudes of public services financed by taxation. These services did not provide the choice or responsiveness that consumers were coming to expect. Even though unemployment was growing in the 1970s, people were becoming more concerned with taxes and prices than jobs. The collectivist concerns with welfare, equality, and employment that were the central values of managed capitalism were giving way to a more individualist focus on freedom and choice.

These changes also help to account for the direction of capitalism's transformation in the 1980s. Managed capitalism had critics on the Left as well as the Right, but in the 1980s it was the right-wing that triumphed. Its so-called 'neo-liberal' beliefs in the freedom of the individual and the free operation of market forces came to dominate ideology and policy. This neo-liberalism sought to reverse the tendencies of managed capitalism and return British society to the vigour of its early capitalist stage. Its main ideas were developed in the 1970s by Keith Joseph, the guru of the New

Right, implemented by governments led by Margaret Thatcher in the 1980s, and then adopted by New Labour in the 1990s.

After the Conservatives' election victory in 1979, both Keynesianism—the maintenance of high employment through the government management of the economy and public spending—and corporatism were out. There was a clear shift of priorities from the maintenance of employment to the control of inflation. The national organizations of the unions and the employers were no longer consulted about government policy and the representatives of both found themselves removed from state bodies. It was no surprise that union representatives were left out in the cold by a government of the Right, but the Director-General of the CBI, the national employers' organization, was shocked to find that he too was cold-shouldered when he met Margaret Thatcher in 1980. The rejection of corporatist relationships cut both ways.

Market forces were to be revived by 'rolling back the state'. Welfare expenditure was cut through the restriction of benefit payments, particularly the payment of unemployment benefit, by the replacement of grants with loans, and by increases in charges. There was, none the less, no overall reduction of state spending, since rising unemployment resulted in higher social security expenditure. Nor was there an overall reduction in taxation but rather a shift from income tax to indirect taxes, which, it was claimed, at least gave people greater choice, since they did not have to buy the products that carried these taxes.

Public sector industries and services were returned to the market-place through various forms of privatization. Its simplest form was the sale of public companies to private individuals and, according to Yergin and Stanislaw, two-thirds of state-owned industries, amounting to forty-six major businesses employing some 900,000 workers, had been sold in this way by 1992. There was also a massive sale of public-sector housing, when council tenants were given the right to buy the property they lived in. Another form it took was 'compulsory competitive tendering'. This required public sector agencies to put the services they supplied out to private tender and give the contract to the most competitive bid. In 1983, for example, all district health authorities were required to introduce competitive tendering for the provision of cleaning, laundry, and catering services. An existing 'in-house' provider might win a contract, but to do so it had to behave like a private company.

Other public sector services could not so easily be privatized. They could, however, be made to behave as though they were competing in a market-place. Thus, the outright privatizing of health and education was not politically possible but the creation of internal markets in health and education forced schools, colleges, and hospitals into competition with each other. At the same time, private alternatives in health and education (and pensions provision too) were subsidized and encouraged. The prison service as a whole was not privatized, but in the 1990s some prisons were placed under private management to generate a competition between private and public sector providers.

Market forces were also revived by removing or reducing the state regulation of economic activities. Deregulation too took many forms, such as the removal of restrictions on Sunday trading, the relaxation of planning regulations, and the lighter touch regulation of commercial television.

Deregulation perhaps had most impact on the financial industry. This had been regulated by the bodies that managed each of its separate areas and maintained the boundaries between them. Building societies and banks, for example, each loaned money but operated in different markets and did not compete with each other. Boundaries between financial functions were out of step with the neo-liberal belief in maximizing competition, though this system was breaking down anyway under the pressures of international competition. London and its financial institutions were competing for capital with New York and other financial centres. The removal of international barriers, especially with the abolition of exchange controls in 1979, intensified these competitive pressures by allowing foreign banks a greater freedom to operate in London and British banks a greater freedom to operate abroad. Barings, whose story we outlined in Chapter 1, used this new freedom opportunistically and disastrously. Financial deregulation speeded the process of financialization, which, as we shall see in Chapter 6, led towards the crisis of 2007.

It must, however, be emphasized that although important deregulatory changes certainly occurred, there was no overall process of deregulation. As Andrew Gamble has forcefully argued, a free economy requires a strong state. The reviving of market forces actually led to more state regulation. There are plentiful examples of this from the Thatcher years.

Privatization alone would not stimulate market competition, if state monopolies were simply turned into private monopolies or private companies were allowed to manipulate markets, so a series of new regulatory 'offices', such as Ofgas, Oftel, and Ofwat, were created to police the gas, telecoms, and water market-places.

In a different way, trade unions were considered to obstruct the free operation of the labour market and were subjected to more legal regulation than they had ever experienced before. They had seen off the 1960s and 1970s attempts by both Labour and Conservative governments to reform them, but in the 1980s they were forced into submission. The legislation that now regulated them was backed by punitive sanctions and defiance could and did lead not only to fines but to a union losing its funds, its buildings, all its assets. The unions took a huge battering from the government in the 1980s, particularly in the carefully planned defeat of the miners' strike in 1984–5 (Figure 5). Coal stocks had been built up before the strike was provoked and the police were

5. Rolling back: the state uses the police to defeat the miners in 1984.

extensively deployed to frustrate the union's picketing tactics and bring miners before the courts. According to Percy-Smith and Hillyard, there were over 4,000 prosecutions, mainly for public order offences.

The central government took tighter control of local government, in order to control overall state expenditure and force the privatization of local government services. In education and health, new state apparatuses for improving and auditing their quality, and providing information about their performance, were constructed. A National Curriculum for state primary and secondary schools was introduced in 1988. There was in fact a greater extension of central state control—over local authorities, education and health, and trade unions—than had ever previously occurred in peace-time Britain. The state was not exactly 'rolled back'!

That all this was not just the result of Conservative government and reflected a new stage in the development of capitalism is shown by the continuation of neo-liberal policies by the Labour governments of 1997–2010. There were departures from the

Thatcherite script, with the introduction of a minimum wage, the granting of recognition rights to the unions, and the redistributive use of tax credits. Most of the extensive legislation regulating union behaviour was, however, left in place, while privatization has been continued rather than reversed. Labour government did make a difference but Labour broadly continued the neo-liberal policies established in the 1980s, especially developing ways of privatizing public services.

This is shown well by Labour's health policies. Labour's 2000 NHS Plan promised one hundred new hospitals by 2010, and 7,500 new consultants, and reduced waiting-times. Patients would be able to choose who treated them and where. Hospitals would compete for patients and money would follow them. League tables would enable patients to exercise choice. This plan clearly manifested neo-liberal values in its emphasis on individual choice and market competition.

The building of new hospitals (and schools and colleges) was financed by the Private Finance Initiative (PFI) method, originating from the previous period of Conservative government but first applied on a large scale by Labour. Hospitals financed in this way found themselves contracted to make payments to private capital for the next 25–30 years, and required to use the expensive services provided by private capital for all maintenance and repairs. According to Allyson Pollock, the payments they had to make were so great that 'for every PFI hospital up and running, equity investors and bankers are charging as if for two'. She argues that the ensuing hospital debts have forced hospital closures and mergers.

Hospitals were encouraged to behave like private corporations. Foundation trusts were introduced in 2002. The plan was that at first only those hospital trusts performing well financially would be granted 'foundation status' but eventually all hospital trusts would achieve it. This status would enable them to raise private capital, pay their staff at higher rates, and contract out health-care freely to private companies. They would be largely freed from supervision by NHS bodies. The drive to achieve this status by the Mid Staffordshire Trust was implicated in the 2009 scandal at Stafford Hospital, where there had been large numbers of deaths due to very poor patient care, as the hospital cut staff in order to save money in pursuit of foundation status. One should, however, note that this particular trust was subsequently abolished, while trusts also came under greater regulation. By the end of 2012 there were 144 foundation trusts.

NHS health-care has been increasingly provided by private companies outside the NHS. In its drive to reduce patient waiting-times, the Labour government introduced privately financed and managed Independent Sector Treatment Centres in 2003. In 2008 the government introduced an Any Qualified Provider Policy, which allowed patients greater choice of private providers. According to the Nuffield Trust study by Arora et al., NHS spending on specialist care by private providers increased sharply after 2006, rising from £4.74 billion in 2006–7 to £8.33 billion in 2011–12.

Fearing the electoral consequences of such an unpopular measure, Margaret Thatcher had held back from privatizing the NHS. Privatization was, however, well under way after the Labour governments of 1997–2010 had brought in the private financing of hospital building, corporate hospital trusts, and extensive private company provision of NHS health care. Health was being remarketized. The Labour Party, now in opposition, has been very critical of the Coalition Government's 2012 Health and Social Care Act, which certainly pushed the privatization process a step further, but had surely paved the way for it.

Transformations of capitalism

In this chapter we have examined two transformations in capitalism. What can we learn about capitalism from them?

The first transformation, from anarchic to managed capitalism, showed that it was possible to protect people from at least some of the worst consequences of the operation of market forces. The conditions of work could be regulated and through collective organization workers could limit the power of the employer and negotiate improvements in wages and conditions. Welfare became a matter for the state, which removed key services from the market-place so that they could be provided equally to all citizens. Governments tried to manage the economy by developing cooperation between the state and the organizations of unions and employers. Capitalism could be managed, even if those trying to manage it often got things wrong, sometimes gave in to pressure from the powerful owners of capital, or simply failed to deliver what they had promised.

The fundamental problem faced by managed capitalism was that in restricting and replacing the market provision of goods and services it was weakening the central mechanism of a capitalist economy. When increasing international competition and the economic problems of the 1970s placed severe strains on the old industrial societies, managed capitalism began to break down. It was also undermined by an increasing individualism that gave greater priority to consumer choice and market provision. There were calls for a return to the values and vitality of earlier times.

In a second transformation market forces were revived, though there was in practice no 'rolling back' of the state, for market mechanisms could only operate in the context of state intervention and regulation. Indeed, the whole notion of an earlier stage in which the market ruled was a myth, for during the time of anarchic capitalism the state had, through the maintenance of order, played a key part in enabling capitalism to function. The latest stage, of remarketized capitalism, has in fact been characterized by a massive increase in state regulation, which in some areas has become more extensive than it ever was during the period of managed capitalism.

The new world of remarketized capitalism provides greater choice and more freedom for the individual but also a less secure life, intensified work pressures, and greater inequality. Whether one considers consumer goods, media channels, holiday destinations, or schools, there is no denying the provision of greater choice. Futures have, however, become less secure, particularly in those critical areas of people's lives—employment, housing, and pensions. Insecurity and the weakening of union organization have reduced the capacity of employees to resist the employers' demands for harder and better work. The gap has widened between those trapped in low-wage occupations who face insecure futures and those able to exploit the new opportunities to accumulate wealth. As managed capitalism developed, the freedom of the individual was diminished in the name of greater equality, but in a remarketized capitalism, equality and security have been sacrificed to freedom and choice.

There is little sign of this changing in the near future, but it would be wrong to assume that this is the final stage in the development of capitalism. If the market now appears unassailable, so did managed capitalism in its time. If managed capitalism had many weaknesses and deficiencies, so does remarketized capitalism, for inequalities and insecurities create their own inefficiencies and pressures for change. Indeed, as we show in Chapter 6, this new stage in the development of capitalism has itself been dogged by instability and recurrent crises. The remarketizing of capitalism has not solved the problems of capitalist society.

Chapter 4
Is capitalism everywhere the same?

As managed capitalism developed in different societies, it took very different organizational and institutional forms, but in the 1980s the neo-liberal model of capitalism became intellectually and ideologically dominant. This model seemed to be driving all societies towards a new market-based uniformity. Does this mean that capitalism is becoming everywhere the same? This chapter examines the development and transformation of three very different systems of managed capitalism in Sweden, the United States, and Japan.

Swedish capitalism

Managed capitalism in Sweden probably comes closest of the three to managed capitalism in Britain. Like Britain it has had a strong labour movement, a highly developed welfare state, and minimal state involvement in the industrialization process, though Sweden was much more successful in developing an efficiently functioning managed capitalism.

The circumstances of Sweden's industrialization were quite different from Britain's. Sweden industrialized later and with only a small domestic market, because of its small population, and its lack of the markets and resources of an overseas empire. Swedish industry was therefore dependent upon exports and had to be highly competitive if it was to survive. Indeed, some have argued that this pressure forced Swedish unions and employers to cooperate and explains the 'labour peace', for which Sweden later became well known.

This view is quite misleading, for there was intense class conflict during the early years of industrial capitalism in Sweden. In 1909 there was a five-month-long general strike that makes the British general strike of 1926, which lasted one whole week, look like a gentlemanly cricket match. The 1909 strike resulted from a steady escalation of conflict, as each side of industry extended its organization in order to outgun the other. Socialists were heavily involved in union organization and in the particular context of Swedish industrialization were able to create a strong and unified organization of the working class. Swedish employers responded by constructing a highly centralized national employers' association, which forced a comparable centralization on the unions. The absence of ethnic and religious divisions and low levels of individualism in a Lutheran society may well have facilitated strong class organization, but conflict was the driving force behind it.

Class cooperation came out of class conflict. The growth of such strong organizations made possible a staunchly corporatist form of managed capitalism, in which its management was substantially delegated to the central organizations. While British governments struggled in the 1950s and 1960s to get the national organizations of the unions and employers to take responsibility for wage restraint, Swedish governments could largely leave this to them. Indeed, Sweden acquired a reputation for 'labour peace' mainly because of the control these powerful organizations exerted over their members. Thus, it was the very intensity of class conflict in Sweden that created the conditions for organized class cooperation and peaceful industrial relations.

A strong and unified labour movement also provided the basis for a long period of Social Democratic government, from 1932 until 1976. This established its reputation through measures to relieve unemployment in the 1930s and an early adoption of Keynesian policies. It later created an advanced and extensive welfare state, based on high and progressive taxation.

State welfare was but one aspect of the collectivist policies of the labour movement. This also strove to reduce inequality through a 'wage solidarity' policy that remarkably compressed wage differentials, with the gap between the average wages of the higher and lower paid halving during the 1960s and 1970s. In the 1970s there was also extensive legislation to protect employees in the workplace and give them a voice in company policy. Such policies were not simply pursued out of ideology. They were part of a Social Democratic strategy to increase the labour movement's organizational and political strength by creating a common interest and identity amongst all employees, working class and middle class.

All this did not mean that Social Democratic Sweden was becoming a non-capitalist society. The labour movement's leadership recognized that welfare depended not just on the strength of socialist ideas and working class organization but also on the operation of a dynamic capitalist economy that could compete internationally and increase the size of the national economic cake. It was one of the central principles of Swedish economic policy that unprofitable companies should be allowed to go bankrupt, so that their resources could be transferred to profitable ones. The union-controlled labour market policy did not protect jobs but assisted workers to become mobile and retrain.

Serious problems afflicted the Social Democratic model in the 1970s. Industrial conflict increased, individualism grew and began to challenge Social Democratic collectivism, while Sweden faced economic crises. A shift of politics to the Right resulted in six years of 'bourgeois' government between 1976 and 1982. The Swedish Right was, however, historically divided between three parties that could not cooperate sufficiently to carry through a Thatcherite transformation. The Social Democrats then returned to government and this, together with more favourable economic conditions, suggested that the Swedish model had weathered the storm.

This was an illusion, for the corporatist cooperation central to the Swedish model was in a state of collapse. Centralized organization had generated its own tensions, not only between centre and periphery but between different sections of labour. The inevitable extension of centralized organization to white-collar and public-sector workers, as their occupations grew, produced very powerful organizations and these then engaged in competitive rivalries, which the centralized structure of Swedish bargaining could not contain and, if anything, amplified. The central wage negotiations became longer, more complex, and more conflictual. In the process Swedish employers became thoroughly alienated from the institutions of central cooperation.

They were also alienated by another sequence of changes. In the 1960s workers became discontented with the impact on their jobs and work conditions of Sweden's dynamic capitalism. A submerged labour radicalism resurfaced with demands for greater industrial and economic democracy. This culminated in the ingenious Meidner Plan to transfer gradually the ownership of industry from private capital to union-controlled funds, though only a heavily watered-down version was actually legislated. The Social Democrat leadership was not going to wreck the capitalist engine of Swedish economic growth. Serious damage was done, none the less, to the relationship between the labour movement and the employers.

The *modus vivendi* established in the 1930s between the labour movement and the employers had come to an end. During the 1980s the main employers' organization embarked on a broad counter-attack to reinstall the values of an individualist and capitalist society. In 1990 the employers finally withdrew from the central wage bargaining that had enabled the reduction of wage differentials. Their strategy switched from a corporatist representation of their interests on state bodies to a greater use of political influence and lobbying.

Swedish capitalism too went through a remarketizing process. The Social Democratic Party itself led this in the 1980s. Welfare capitalism had generated a large public sector, high public expenditure, a large government deficit, and inflationary wage settlements, which were evidently eroding Swedish competitiveness. Business leaders warned that unless changes were made they would have to move their operations out of Sweden and the leadership of the Social Democratic Party recognized that industry was becoming uncompetitive. Exchange controls were lifted and financial markets deregulated; private capital was brought into state-owned industries; local authority services were operated increasingly on business lines; benefits and public expenditure were cut; taxation became increasingly indirect.

This was only the start of the process and more recently Sweden has embarked on thoroughgoing neo-liberal reforms that have made it the toast of neo-liberals. After its victory in 2006 the right-wing Moderate Party at last succeeded in constructing a 'bourgeois' coalition government capable of carrying out effective neo-liberal policies. Public spending and taxes were sharply reduced. Public spending, which had reached 67 per cent of GNP in 1993 had been cut to 49 per cent by 2011. Austerity was institutionalized in a law requiring governments to achieve a 1 per cent budget surplus over each business cycle. There were cuts in unemployment benefit, sick pay, and pensions. There was a loss of important employment rights. There was further privatization of education, health services, and the care of the old. The trade unions came under financial attack, as the government made membership of unions and the union-controlled unemployment benefit funds more expensive.

Sweden has long been seen as a relatively egalitarian society. What impact has remarketization had here? According to a 2011 OECD report, 'the growth in inequality between 1985 and the late 2000s was the largest among all OECD countries, increasing by one third.' Sweden still, however, 'belongs to the group of nine most equal OECD countries' (out of thirty-four). Sweden is also 'the highest spender on public services such as education, health or care among the OECD'. So although Sweden had been rushing to join the neo-liberal club, it was still a *relatively* egalitarian country in 2008 (the year of the OECD data).

Is Sweden now no different to any other remarketized capitalist society? It does remain relatively collectivist. Central wage agreements no longer exist but their replacement by broad industry-level agreements between employer and union groupings shows that Swedish wage bargaining has remained coordinated, while some central agreements on non-wage matters, such as pensions and redundancy arrangements, are still negotiated. Union membership has declined but is still, internationally speaking, exceptionally high, with 67.5 per cent of employees unionized in 2012, as compared with 26 per cent in Britain. Collective bargaining remains at a very high level, with some 90 per cent of workers covered by collective bargaining in Sweden, as compared with 29 per cent in Britain. Consistent with this higher collective organization is the greater protection of employees from dismissal, which, according to the OECD, remains relatively high in Sweden, and much higher than in Britain. Employee representation on company boards, as legislated in 1987, also continues.

So what does the Swedish case tell us about capitalism? It shows that in certain conditions the conflict between employers and unions generated by capitalism can provide the basis for centralized class cooperation and a functioning system of corporatist management and welfare capitalism. It also shows that such a system could not in the end contain the underlying conflicts between capital and labour, and between sections of labour, which eventually paralysed it. Increasing international competition and global economic integration then made such a high-cost system impossible to maintain, and Sweden eventually conformed to international neo-liberal tendencies. This did not mean, however, that the structures and institutions created during the period of managed capitalism disappeared. The revitalizing of Swedish capitalism has not eliminated its collectivist distinctiveness.

American capitalism

With its pronounced individualism, American capitalism has been at the opposite end of the ideological and organizational spectrum. Industrialization occurred in a decentralized and individualist society, where there was a widespread belief in success through enterprise and initiative. The absence of an aristocracy and the establishment of political and civil rights by the 18th-century American Revolution had encouraged such beliefs. The growth of industrial capitalism did result in the formation of unions, but these were mainly self-interested organizations of craft workers that were not concerned with class organization or the socialist transformation of society.

In this context the business corporation flourished and produced a corporate rather than corporatist capitalism, in which business corporations rather than class organizations were the dominant actors. The large American domestic market enabled the growth of big corporations and in the late 19th century a greater concentration of ownership occurred than in other industrial societies. At first this took the form of 'horizontal' mergers to give control over markets, as in Rockefeller's construction of Standard Oil. It was, however, the 'vertically' integrated corporation, which built a strong and secure competitive position by bringing together all stages in the production and distribution of a product, that became the dominant form in the 20th century.

America was the home of the 'managerial revolution' theory, discussed briefly in Chapter 3. Alfred Chandler has argued that the managers of American corporations were distinctively allowed to 'get on with the job' during the period of corporate growth, which largely resulted from their highly developed 'organizational capabilities'. He contrasted American management, with its use of profits to finance investment and growth, with the more personal and traditional ownership of British companies, which were more concerned with dividends to shareholders than long-term investment.

The centrality of the business corporation was paralleled by the distinctive character of American trade unionism. This was predominantly a 'business unionism' concerned with obtaining the best possible contract for union members. They obtained not only good wages but also fringe benefits, such as holidays-with-pay, insurance, and health care, particularly after the Second World War. This business unionism was limited in extent and the proportion of employees unionized barely topped one-third at its peak in 1954.

As the importance of fringe benefits shows, some of the welfare that in Europe was the province of the state was in America provided by the corporation. Indeed, the term 'welfare capitalism' in America refers to corporate welfare provision. This is not to say that there was no development of state welfare in America, but this only provided a piecemeal safety-net for the poor. Welfare was otherwise the responsibility of the corporation or the individual, and was delivered by private services operating through the market-place.

Individualism and free market ideologies did not keep the state out of economic life. On the contrary, the monopolistic tendencies of business corporations meant that economic life required regulation, if competition were to be maintained and the interests of consumers protected. An 'anti-trust' movement emerged in the late 19th century and the Sherman Act of 1890 declared illegal any activity or organization 'in restraint of trade or commerce'. This did not stop the growth of powerful corporations, but it did have consequences, notably forcing the break-up of Standard Oil. It gave rise to a distinctively American apparatus of anti-trust legislation and enforcement. The state had been drawn into economic life not by class conflict, as in Europe, but to protect the market.

In the 1930s state intervention appeared to take a much more European direction. In response to the Great Depression, Franklin Roosevelt's New Deal legislated ambitious relief and welfare programmes, eventually adopting Keynesian economic policies. It came into considerable conflict with big business over its taxation proposals; its drive to provide, partly through the publicly owned Tennessee Valley Authority, cheap electricity; its continuation of the 'anti-trust' attack on monopolistic tendencies; and its legislation to protect trade unions.

Unions were given the right to organize and bargain collectively, and a National Labour Relations Board was set up to enforce these rights. Union membership tripled between 1933 and 1938, as the Committee for Industrial Organization (CIO) established a more inclusive trade unionism and organized America's mass production industries. Further legislation to regulate wages and hours of work, and protect vulnerable groups, was passed in 1938.

However, the federal structure of the state, and its fragmenting division of powers between President, Congress, and Supreme

Court, gave opponents many opportunities to block and frustrate New Deal measures. Furthermore, although the New Deal created an astonishing range of agencies and programmes, it lacked coherence, at least in comparison with the more ideological programmes developed in Europe. It depended on the commitment and energy of Roosevelt and an army of well-intentioned and highly motivated reformers and administrators. There was no reformist political party to support it. The pro-labour legislation of the 1930s was at least partly reversed by the Taft-Hartley Act of 1947, which substantially weakened the unions' powers and rights.

In other respects, the managed capitalism of the New Deal continued to operate during the 1950s and 1960s. The social security legislation and welfare programmes introduced in the 1930s were extended in the 1950s and 1960s, especially to give free medical care to the poor and the old. As late as the 1970s, during Richard Nixon's presidency, the federal government experimented with the control of prices and incomes. Deficit financing continued with first the Second World War and then the Cold War resulting in massive military expenditure. The profitability of substantial sections of industry, and therefore the employment and earnings of labour, depended on state spending. The whole idea of a state-directed industrial policy was anathema in the United States, but, as David Coates has argued, the creation of a military–industrial complex was, in effect, one form of such a policy. Business opposed government interference but accepted government money.

While American industry was in better competitive shape than British industry, it too suffered in the later 1960s and 1970s from inherited rigidities and intensified international competition, especially from Japan. Lower levels of trade unionism, state welfare, and public ownership did mean that there was less pressure for transformation than in Britain but the United States too went through a process of neo-liberal change.

In the 1980s and 1990s, American society was remarketized to some degree. The Reagan administration of the early 1980s sought to stimulate market forces by cutting both taxes and government expenditure, though vested interests resisted cuts in the latter and the budget deficit actually increased. The deregulation of the airlines marked the first break with the New Deal tradition of industrial regulation and was followed by the deregulation of the railways, of trucking, telecommunications, and electricity generation. The publicly owned part of the railways, and many state-run local services and prisons, were privatized. A welfare-to-work programme, which became a model for New Labour in Britain, limited the duration of welfare payments and forced recipients into low-paid work.

As in Britain, these changes were accompanied by the greater exploitation of labour. Hours of work lengthened and real wages dropped at the rate of 1 per cent a year during the 1980s. Industrial corporations moved their plants south from the 'rust belt' to the 'sun belt' and then Mexico, in search of cheaper labour. Elitist 'business unions' concerned with meeting the immediate needs of their existing members either failed to organize the new labour force or (in Mexico) could not. By 2001 union density had dropped to a very low 13 per cent of the labour force.

Inequality increased. Thomas Piketty has described an 'explosion of inequality', which after the 1970s returned the United States to the level of income inequality previously reached in the 1920s (Figure 6). He sees this as a result of the 'supersalaries' earned by 'supermanagers', who effectively set their own salaries through their control of the corporations they headed. A gap has opened up between this group and the middle class, let alone those further down the scale. International comparisons, based on data from the Luxembourg Income Study reported by David Leonhardt and Kevin Quealy, show that this gap has become greater in the US than in comparable countries. Those at the top are doing

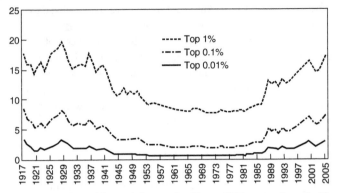

6. The American rich get richer, again. Share of US pre-tax household income received by the top 1 percent, top 0.1 percent, and top 0.01 percent, between 1917 and 2005.

better than their counterparts elsewhere, while those lower down are falling further behind.

Other important changes in management reversed the 'managerial revolution' of the early 20th century. The greater mobility of capital, popular investment in the stock market, and the expansion of the financial services industry increased the importance of a company's market valuation. According to the newly fashionable doctrine of 'shareholder value', the goal of management was no longer to invest in the future or build up a company but only to maximize its share price by increasing profits. Managers were given an incentive to do this through stock options which rewarded them for increases in their company's share price. Managers had been at least to some extent separated from owners by the managerial revolution, but now they increasingly became owners again.

The focus on shareholder value could lead companies to divert their operations into complex financial activities and the fraudulent inflation of their share prices. Enron started in 1985 as a company engaged in energy distribution but then diversified into trading over 800 commodities and financial products. It borrowed large sums from investment banks, which recommended its stock to their clients, and it inflated its profits through fraudulent accountancy, eventually going bust in 2001. In another famous scandal, WorldCom, which started as a small Mississippi phone company in 1983, bought sixty companies in financially complex transactions, engaged in accountancy fraud to inflate its profits, and went bust in 2002.

Investment banks were also heavily implicated in the dot.com bubble that burst in 2000, by launching and floating internet companies, pushing up their stock prices, making money from their holdings and all the financial activities that this process involved. It was the ordinary investors who paid the price when the bubble burst.

These scandals and malpractices were blamed on the behaviour of deviant individuals or the foolishness of investors. Geoffrey Ingham has argued that they were actually symptomatic of 'the financialization of modern capitalism in the sense of the increasing dominance of financial practices and the fusion of business enterprise with financial engineering'. American capitalism was transformed by financialization during the last quarter of the 20th century. At a time when companies engaged in production were facing growing competition from abroad and struggling to make profits, financial activities were highly profitable and attracted capital.

Indeed, it was arguably in this area that the remarketizing of American capitalism had its most significant consequences through the deregulation of financial activities. American banks were ingeniously creating many new financial products, such as 'derivatives', of the kind that Nick Leeson traded (see Chapter 1). Derivatives were initially banned by the regulatory authorities, which regarded trading in them as illegal gambling activities, but under Wall Street pressure regulations were changed or lifted to allow this to take place.

The repeal of the 1932 Banking Act marked the victory of neo-liberal deregulation. This Act had been passed to separate commercial from investment banking. By the late 1970s, under pressure from the banks, the Act was being reinterpreted to allow commercial banks to invest in derivatives. It was increasingly argued that the Act's restrictions weakened the international competitiveness of American banks. In 1999 it was repealed.

Thus America too had travelled from a managed to a remarketized capitalism. Managed capitalism in America was importantly different to managed capitalism in Britain and Sweden—collective organization was less extensive, state welfare less universal, anti-trust legislation stronger—but America did, none the less, go through this stage. The transition to remarketized capitalism certainly occurred in the sphere of production but was arguably most prominent in the financial sphere, which had become ever larger as capital went into financial activities. This was a remarkable change as America shifted from being the globally dominant producer of manufactured goods, most famously in the assembly-line production of cars, to being the leading innovator in financial products.

It was apparently a very successful shift, as large profits were made from financial activities and the economy as a whole grew, but there was far more risk in these activities than their practitioners realized and they were building up dangerous levels of debt, as we shall see in Chapter 6.

Japanese capitalism

Japanese industrial capitalism was managed from its very beginnings. By the middle of the 19th century Japan was a highly commercialized and entrepreneurial society but not yet an industrial one. After the Meiji Restoration, Japan's 19th-century revolution, industrialization was directed by the state as part of a programme to build a strong and independent country that could stand up to the Western empires encroaching upon Japan. The individualism and liberalism of the West were attractive to some thinkers but alien to Japan's new rulers, who were nationalist bureaucrats schooled in the Japanese version of Confucianism.

The new government tried to industrialize Japan by setting up model state enterprises but these ran into such difficulties that in the 1880s the government privatized those that were not of military importance. Privatization did not, however, mean that Japanese industry now consisted of independent private companies. Large industrial groupings known as *zaibatsu* emerged—Mitsubishi, Mitsui, Sumitomo, and Yasuda. They were owned by families, which controlled them through holding companies. Corporate concentration was occurring in all industrial societies but in Japan it took a unique form, for each *zaibatsu* stretched across virtually the whole of Japanese industry and had its own bank and its own trading company to market its products. The *zaibatsu* were closely connected with the state and eventually performed important colonial functions for the government.

The model enterprises were anyway the least important aspect of the state's promotion of economic growth. The government removed feudal barriers and restrictions to create a modern nation-state. Japan became a unified country, while the heavy subsidizing of railways and shipping transformed communications. Shipbuilding too was heavily subsidized and by 1939 Japan's production here was second only to Britain's. The state also created a banking system to finance investment and trade, with specialized banks to meet the needs of the various parts of the economy.

Skills were rapidly imported from the West. Japan exemplifies Thomas Piketty's dictum that 'the diffusion of knowledge and skills' has been the 'main force in favour of greater equality between countries'. But Japan also went a key step further in replacing foreign experts with home-produced ones. A national educational system was created which by the beginning of the 20th century was already in advance of Britain's, even though Japan was far less developed economically.

The state maintained Japan's economic independence. Foreign capital was kept out, until Japan had become a strong independent state. Indeed, it was the peasantry that bore the main cost of Japan's modernization through a land tax that initially provided three-quarters of the government's income. Japan also began to construct an overseas empire that would provide it with protected markets and raw materials.

Japan was the only non-Western society to industrialize successfully in the 19th century. A distinctive managed capitalism had been created, in which the state played a directive role and corporate concentration took the form of industrial groups that stretched across the economy. Another distinctive feature was the weakness of labour organization. Workers did try to organize, with some success during the First World War, when industry boomed and labour was in high demand, but met heavy employer opposition and state repression. State welfare too was undeveloped, in part because employers preferred to introduce company welfare schemes that integrated workers and detached them from the labour movement.

These distinctive features were further developed during the postwar period, when Japan's growth machine really got going and made the Japanese economy the second largest in the world. The *zaibatsu* were dismantled but then reconstructed. Mitsubishi, like Krupp in Germany, was now seen as an anti-communist resource rather than a reservoir of fascism. Crucially, the *zaibatsu* were rebuilt under the aegis of the Ministry of Trade and Industry (MITI), the powerhouse of the state's industrial policy, which used its control of trade, currency, and investment to develop the industries of the future.

The reconstructed *zaibatsu* and other similar groupings performed important economic functions. They provided coordination across industrial boundaries but also engaged in intense competition, which stimulated productivity and enhanced international competitiveness. They could pursue long-term policies aimed at building market-share, because their reconstruction on the basis of mutual ownership and their finance by the banks relieved them of shareholder pressure for high dividends. This also meant that they were protected from take-overs by foreign capital or corporate raiders. This pattern of ownership was linked to integration within the company, for Japanese companies could look after their employees instead of maximizing the payment of dividends to shareholders.

Union organization grew rapidly during the first years of the Occupation, giving the lie to claims that Japanese unions have been weak for cultural reasons. In January 1946 there were 900,000 union members, but by June 1949 there were over 6.5 million, as compared with the prewar peak membership of 421,000 in 1936. They were at first encouraged as 'democratic' organizations by the Occupation Authority, but this rapid growth, in the context of its policy shift from an anti-fascist to an anti-communist stance, led to a sustained and violent attack on them by both employers and the state. The employer strategy soon became, however, not the destruction of unions as such but their replacement with tame 'enterprise unions'. At the 'battle of Nissan' in 1953 the company, backed by the Japanese Employers' Association and with financial support from the banks, provoked the existing union into a strike, locked out its members, created its own Nissan union, and gave those who joined it their jobs back. Enterprise unions became the norm.

High employee integration gave Japanese companies the edge that enabled them to out-compete their Western rivals. The company provided the security of lifetime employment, wages that increased with seniority and length of service, welfare services, and often housing. In return employees had to work hard and long, giving up weekends and holidays if required by their company. Other mechanisms of integration were the absence of status distinctions within the company, company uniforms, and the social interaction of workers and managers both at work and leisure. Earnings differentials have been very much lower in Japanese companies than comparable Western ones.

Integration for some was at the expense of others. Contract workers, part-time workers, and women workers did not enjoy the benefits of lifetime employment and all that went with it. This also applied to the small companies subcontracted to carry out much more of the large company's work than in Western industrial societies. These were the shock-absorbers that enabled the large companies to ride out economic fluctuations by turning labour on and off as required. There was a sharp division in Japan between an integrated elite of permanent employees and a disposable periphery.

A key set of linkages in a highly integrated institutional structure operated through the Japanese welfare system. There was only a rudimentary welfare state, which kept workers highly dependent on company welfare schemes and reinforced their subservience but also encouraged the Japanese to save privately for a 'rainy day'. Individual savings went into a postal savings scheme controlled by the state, which could then channel them into industries marked out for investment.

So, in Japan there was an undeniably successful capitalism very different in character to the others we have examined. While the welfare state has been an integral part of Swedish capitalism, its absence was crucial to the Japanese model. The state's directive role has been particularly distinctive, and led some commentators to call for Western governments to develop comparable industrial policies. Patterns of corporate ownership and bank finance contrast with the stock-market model of the United Kingdom and the United States. Company domination of workers has been more complete in Japan than even the United States, where unions have been more combative. Company welfare too has been more extensive, and Ronald Dore has described Japanese capitalism as a 'welfare capitalism' in yet another application of this label.

Like the other systems of managed capitalism that we have examined, the Japanese one ran into difficulties in the later 1960s and the 1970s, when Japan also came under heavy and steady external pressure to open itself up to trade. This really began after the early 1970s rapprochement between the United States and China changed the American view of Japan, which was now regarded not so much as a bulwark against East Asian communism but as an industrial competitor that engaged systematically in unfair trade practices. Although Japan found ways of replacing tariff with non-tariff barriers, famously declaring that Raleigh bicycles made in Britain were unsafe, restrictions on the import of goods and capital were gradually lifted. MITI's instruments of control were dismantled and it had to rely increasingly on 'administrative guidance' through its extensive network of retired bureaucrats with second careers in industry.

Japan did not, however, respond to the problems of the 1970s by abandoning its institutions and plunging down a neo-liberal path. Growth and international competitiveness were sustained by exporting the capital accumulated through growth and setting up operations to exploit cheaper labour abroad, particularly in South-East Asia, but also in Europe, the United States, and Australia. MITI launched a new drive to develop the knowledge-based industries of the future, and Japan soon became the world's leading producer of microchips. So strong was the competitive strength of Japanese industry that the United States continued through the 1980s to run a huge trade deficit with Japan, though Japanese investment in American bonds recycled some of Japan's earnings back to the United States and financed its deficit.

All this changed at the beginning of the 1990s. Share and land prices had reached unsustainable heights and the bubbles burst. A stock-market crash was followed by economic stagnation and higher unemployment. Japan entered a vicious deflationary circle. As unemployment rose and uncertainty about the future increased, people saved more, consumer demand dropped, and growth declined even further.

The institutions that had enabled growth now attracted criticism. Lifetime employment was viewed as a 'rigidity' that interfered with the free workings of a labour market and prevented companies shedding labour. Mutual ownership in the industrial groups was criticized for supporting unprofitable companies and preventing a refreshing inflow of capital from abroad. The banks were considered too closely linked with industrial groups and therefore unable to pull the plug on unprofitable companies. Faltering economic growth and the exposure of corrupt links between companies, banks, political parties, and bureaucrats combined to undermine the 'developmental state'. Inside and outside Japan, there were calls for Japan to conform to the market model that, it was claimed, the pressures of globalization in any case made unavoidable.

Change has certainly occurred in the labour market. While, as Yoshio Sugimoto has put it 'the familial and paternalistic Japanese-style model remains entrenched in Japan's work culture', there has been a 'casualization of the workforce' and the introduction of 'performance-based employment'. In 2008 a third of the labour force consisted of non-regular employees, largely part-time, contract, and temporary workers. Increasingly pay has been determined not by seniority but by performance, which is less positive than it sounds, since it can mean very long working hours without the payment of overtime. According to Jeff Kingston, 'in the twenty-first century there has been rapid growth in the ranks of the working poor in Japan'.

Japan has also come under growing pressure to allow a greater mobility of capital and deregulate financial markets. The so-called 'big bang' deregulation of banking and finance announced in 1996 has allowed Japanese capital greater freedom and facilitated the entry of foreign financial interests. Some bankruptcies and rationalization followed, as weak institutions lost their protection. Foreign capital started to move in, Renault taking over a failing Nissan in 1999 and closing some of its factories. According to Bruce Aronson, a strong capital market of the kind found in the US or the UK has not, however, developed in Japan and traditional banking practices have continued. While this may mean that Japan has not benefited much from the entrepreneurial activities of venture capital, it has also meant that Japan has largely escaped the financialization that led Western economies into the 2007–8 crisis.

Japan was starting to remarketize its economy but not enough to spring it out of the deflation that had dogged it since the 1990s. There were government attempts to inject money into the economy but Japan's growth-rate remained very low, its GDP rising at only 0.2 per cent a year between 1991 and 2012. One consequence of deflation and declining tax revenues was the accumulation of a huge public debt, which had reached 230 per cent of GDP in 2012. Considered unsustainable by many, this was, David Pilling points out, not as bad as it might appear to be, since at least 90 per cent of it is owed to Japanese savers rather than foreign lenders.

Japan was, indeed, far from being the basket-case that some foreign commentators have called it. Its major corporations have continued to dominate international trade. Unemployment had risen above 5 per cent in 2002 but this was still, internationally speaking, a low rate and had dropped under 4 per cent in early 2014. David Pilling points out that if one considers *real per capita income*, thereby taking account of the beneficial effects of deflation on prices and Japan's relatively static population size, Japan has actually performed better than Britain and the United States since 2002. He also points out that in the last thirty years the benefits of growth have gone almost entirely to the top 1 per cent of earners in the UK and the US but have been 'more evenly distributed' in Japan.

What does the future hold? Shinzo Abe, the Prime Minister of Japan at the time of writing, is making the most determined government effort since the 1990 crash to break out of deflation. Abe is known both for his Abenomics, and for his nationalist/militarist stand against an increasingly powerful China. The two are not unrelated, since Abe clearly makes the connection between national and economic strength. His plan to catapult Japan out of deflation was to fire 'three arrows'.

The first two, a big increase in government spending and a burst of quantitative easing (QE) have already been deployed. QE has led to a fall of the yen, which has benefited the big export corporations, though at the cost of increasing economic conflict with China, which may well retaliate. Inflation has indeed resulted but the spending power of ordinary people has not risen sufficiently to generate the higher demand the economy needs, partly because VAT has been increased in a bid to reduce public sector debt. The third and remarketizing arrow of ambitious structural reform, focusing particularly on the labour market, medical services, and farming, has inevitably met resistance from highly organized interests. Abenomics has its own problems and contradictions.

Remarketization has been gradually occurring but Japan is well known for its cultural and institutional continuities. Japan has also, however, experienced great transformations in the past, notably during the Meiji Restoration and the postwar military occupation of the later 1940s. Change is once again in the air. Even before Abenomics appeared on the scene, Jeff Kingston considered that there were clear signs of transformation in response to the 'lost decade' of the 1990s.

In both the previous great transformations the impact of the outside world played a key part. Will Shinzo Abe push a further transformation through, under pressure from the growing power of China? If he does, this does not mean that Japanese distinctiveness will disappear. This is, after all, the lesson of the earlier transformations, which created distinctive and effective institutions by fusing the old and the new.

Convergence?

We have examined the emergence of three national systems of managed capitalism with distinctive organizations and institutions. In all three, capitalist industrialization generated class organization and class conflict, and attempts by governments to manage the problems of a capitalist society. Each also created its own 'welfare capitalism', though this meant different things in each society.

Although each seemed to have solved the problems of capitalism in its own way, all three faced growing problems from the 1970s, in part because of changes in the world economy but in part because of the problems that their distinctive institutions had created. All came under pressure to abandon their practices of managed capitalism and introduce reforms that would allow market forces greater freedom to operate. All three have gone through a process of remarketization. But does this mean that their national differences have been disappearing as they have all adopted the same practices?

The first point to make here is that models come and go. All three countries have at one time or another been considered by at least some people as the leading capitalist economy which others should emulate. Indeed, it was thought that their success would make it inevitable that others would have to follow the same path. Yet each national set of institutions generated its own problems and each economy ended up in crisis. Most recently, the free market and shareholder capitalism of the United States seemed to be all-conquering but it was this capitalism that led to scandals galore and the long crisis that started in 2007.

Increased international competition and globalization have resulted in remarketization in all three countries but this should not be confused with convergence, for each capitalism has remarketized at its own speed in its own way. Furthermore, distinctive national institutions confer their own specialized advantages as countries compete. Lastly, although the term 'globalization' refers to important changes in capitalism, notably the increased volume and speed of movements of capital, it carries with it a misleading notion of global homogenization, as Chapter 5 will show.

Chapter 5
Has capitalism gone global?

The words 'global capitalism' have become commonplace and there is much to suggest that capitalism is now organized on a global basis. Huge sums of money are transmitted across the world on a daily basis. Companies run manufacturing operations in many different countries in distant parts of the world. Markets for goods and services, for capital and labour too, are in many ways global in extent. These are the realities of a global capitalism that impacts daily on people's lives, but there are also many myths associated with this notion. In this chapter we explore both the realities and the myths.

Global capitalism old and new

A first myth is that global capitalism is something new. Almost as soon as it had come into existence, capitalism spread across the world. The navigators of the 15th and 16th centuries, who piloted the routes from Europe to other continents, were quickly followed by merchant capitalists. The East India companies brought the products of Asia to the consumers of Europe and exported their manufactures in return. The Atlantic trade triangle shipped goods from Europe to Africa, sold slaves from Africa to the Americas and the Caribbean, and took back to Europe the sugar, rum, and cotton they produced.

Travel was, however, slow, intermittent, and hazardous until the communications revolution of the 19th century, which was quite as profound as the one that we have recently been living through. It was not only that steam-powered trains and ships speeded up travel, they also enabled the mass transportation of goods and people across the world, and on a regular and reliable basis independent of the weather. The invention of the telegraph meant that messages no longer had to be carried by people or pigeons, and after the laying of submarine telegraph cables London could communicate with Australia in four days rather than the seventy taken by surface mail. The later invention of the telephone for the first time 'destroyed distance' by making possible instant communication across the world.

It was also in the 19th century that an organized global economy came into existence. Its central principle was an international division of labour between a small group of manufacturing nations and the rest of the world, which became a market for their goods and the source of the food and raw materials they could not provide for themselves. Capital moved freely between countries but within the framework provided by the gold standard, which after 1870 increasingly regulated the relationships between national economies. It did this by fixing the value of currencies in relation to gold, until this standard disintegrated under the pressures generated by the 1930s depression.

This global economy was organized within empires that were extensions of the nation-states at their core. These empires took the form not only of colonial territories but also of spheres of influence that divided up areas of the world not under direct colonial control. While European states first created overseas empires, the United States constructed its own less formal empire in the Pacific and Latin America, and in the last quarter of the 19th century Japan began to follow the European model and acquire its first overseas territories. Under the pressure of international competition and the economic crises of the early

20th century, the world became increasingly divided by imperial boundaries, as each country tried to protect its overseas markets and supplies. After the First World War the movement towards growing global economic integration actually went into reverse.

After the Second World War this imperial framework began to collapse. New centres of finance and production could now emerge outside the old industrial nations. Trade flowed not within national/imperial borders but across them. Both capital and labour began to move more freely across frontiers. Global capitalism may not have been new but it was certainly transformed and entered a phase of exceptional dynamism.

Global manufacturing

While the international division of labour prevailed, wage labour was mainly concentrated in the industrial societies. It certainly existed in the mines, the plantations, and the commercial agriculture of the Third World but in localized pockets, often in an intermediate or intermittent form, combined with other ways of making a living through peasant agriculture or trading activities. According to David Coates, capital's search for labour has doubled the size of the 'world proletariat' to some 3 billion people during the last thirty years of the 20th century.

The main vehicle of the spread of capitalist production has been the transnational corporation. There was a particularly fast growth of these corporations during the last quarter of the 20th century, with their numbers increasing from 7,000 in 1973 to 26,000 in 1993. Their investment in operations abroad rose particularly rapidly after 1985. Although much of this went into other industrial societies, investment in developing countries mounted sharply in the 1990s.

One of the best examples of this process is the growth of manufacturing plants, known as *maquiladoras,* in Mexico. This began when in 1965 Mexico allowed factories within ten miles of its border with the United States to import raw materials and parts duty-free, if the finished product was re-exported. Their growth accelerated after the 1993 NAFTA Agreement removed the remaining barriers to trade. American, European, and eventually Japanese capital moved in to exploit cheap Mexican labour. Thousands of manufacturing and assembly plants, mainly in the vehicle, electronic, and textiles industries, were set up along the border. Managers came in by car daily from their homes in the United States, while carless workers were bussed in from shanty towns.

Labour was cheap there not only because of its plentiful supply but also because it was unorganized and unregulated. Attempts to create independent trade unions were crushed by the combined efforts of employers and government. The NAFTA Agreement contained rights for workers and protection for unions but these parts of it have not been implemented. American unions with an obvious interest in reducing the competition from cheap labour in Mexico tried to organize Mexican workers and invoke the labour clauses of NAFTA but without much success. Health, safety, and environmental regulations were non-existent or very weakly enforced. The Mexican government had a clear interest in turning a blind eye, since the *maquiladoras* made a major contribution to the Mexican economy by providing employment, around a million jobs at the beginning of this century, and making the second largest contribution, after oil, to foreign exchange earnings.

Asia has more recently provided an even bigger attraction to capital, especially Japanese capital, which moved in a series of waves into the countries of the Far East. Production in Japan became increasingly expensive as the rapid growth of Japanese industry after the Second World War led to shortages of land and labour, and prices rose at home. In the 1970s and 1980s Japanese capital moved in search of cheaper labour into the 'tiger economies' of Hong Kong, Taiwan, Singapore, and South Korea. As production became more expensive there, a second wave of capital moved from Japan and the 'tigers' into Indonesia, Malaysia, and Thailand. More recently a third wave of investment has gone into China and Vietnam.

The spread of manufacturing into these countries has particularly drawn young women into wage labour (Figure 7). They reportedly constituted some 60–70 per cent of the *maquiladora* labour force in Mexico. The Nike and Gap factories in South-East Asia have been accused of employing girls under the age of 16, in spite of laws and guidelines prohibiting the exploitation of child labour. Capitalism combines with patriarchy to obtain the cheapest labour, for women are generally paid less than men, subject to male control, and disposable, since they can be returned to the household if the demand for labour drops.

This spread of wage labour has weakened labour in the old industrial societies. Workers there have not only lost good jobs, they have also lost bargaining power. Collective organization had enabled workers to reduce the power differential between capital and labour. Competition from cheap and unregulated labour abroad has undermined this collective power and unions have found it very difficult to extend labour organization to include overseas workers, who, broadly speaking, remain unorganized.

There has been some compensation, since, as consumers, workers in the old industrial societies have certainly benefited. Cheaper labour abroad and greater international competition lowered the prices of the goods that they bought. This meant that *real* wages in Britain actually continued to increase until very recently, though the rate of increase has been falling. According to the Office for National Statistics, the annual rate of increase in real wages fell from 2.9 per cent in the 1980s, to 1.5 per cent in the 1990s, and 1.2 per cent in the 2000s. During 2010–13 real wages actually decreased by 2.2 per cent annually.

7. Cheap labour for Nike in Vietnam.

Global telework

It is not only manufacturing that has moved out of the old industrial societies, for most office work, such as typing, telephone-answering, data-processing, software development and problem-solving, can now be done at a distance. Advances in information and communication technology have made it particularly easy to transfer this kind of work to cheaper locations abroad, where wages and office costs are much lower. As with manufacturing and for the same reasons, it is commonly young women who are employed in this work.

Call-centres were at one time Britain's fastest growing source of employment, replacing the jobs lost in manufacturing, but then these jobs in turn were moved overseas. Banks, insurance companies, travel agencies, telecom and rail companies transferred call-centre operations from Britain to China, India, and Malaysia. Similarly, French companies moved jobs of this kind to Francophone countries in Africa. American companies have long since moved call-centre and data-processing work to the Caribbean.

It is a considerable advantage to be in an English-speaking part of the world, which has given some Caribbean islands and India a head start, though having English alone is not enough. Some training is, of course, needed and those working in telephone-answering services in India are trained in Western pronunciation and conversation. Effective call-centre operations also need careful management by 'relationship managers', who can strike a balance between efficiency considerations and customer service. Software development requires higher-level skills. The city of Bangalore in India became a major centre of software production, because of the availability of a highly educated, English-speaking workforce. Such high-profile companies as Texas Instruments, Motorola, Hewlett Packard, and IBM set up software (and hardware) production there.

This is not only a matter of poor countries providing cheaper labour than rich countries but also of intense competition between the poor countries themselves. Barbados and Jamaica, where telework has long been established, met a growing competition from other Caribbean islands and Central America. The Caribbean as a whole faced competition from the even cheaper labour available in India, the Philippines, Malaysia, and China. The ease with which telework operations can be set up means that there are few limits to the spread of its more routine and low-skilled forms.

Global tourism

International tourism is not often mentioned in accounts of the global spread of capitalism, but its growth is one of the most striking manifestations of the increasing economic connections between countries. Between 1950 and 2013 international tourist arrivals increased from 25 million a year to over 1.087 billion. Tourism has become the main earner of foreign exchange in many of the world's poorest countries.

International tourism spreads capitalist practices into parts of the world that have been little touched historically by the growth of capitalism. It can penetrate into areas that have little capacity to produce goods or other services for the world market. Indeed, remote or undeveloped places, from Macchu Pichu on the eastern slopes of the Andes to Himalayan kingdoms, can be particularly attractive to tourists because they are remote or traditional. Tourism then creates employment in paid labour in bar and hotel work. It generates a greater demand for food production and transport, and may well provide the basis for the local manufacturing of souvenirs and faking of relics. The earnings from tourism can increase the circulation of money, lead to the import of manufactured goods, and establish new consumption patterns.

A process of commodification takes place as cultural practices, wildlife, sights, and views acquire a monetary value that they never had before. Customs may lose their authenticity when commercialized and nature may become less natural but commercialization can at least enable their survival in a modified form. In an increasingly capitalist world, the only way of ensuring the survival of cultural practices and natural sights is to find ways of making a profit out of them. Furthermore, the preservation principle can itself become the basis of an industry, as in the eco-tourism promoted by Costa Rica.

Global tourism has also been responsible for another process of commodification through sex tourism, as the bodies of both adults and children in poor countries acquire a monetary value. The scale of sex tourism is huge. It was reported in 1999 that in the United States alone more than twenty-five companies offered sex tours to Asian destinations. International sex guides provide information and reports on the availability, services, and prices of sex workers in every country in the world, with links to help people make their travel arrangements.

Global tourism is clearly not an unmixed blessing, and even if it does bring some economic rewards to the societies receiving the tourists, one must bear in mind that much of the profit is expatriated by the foreign-owned corporations—airlines, hotel chains, and travel companies—that dominate this trade.

Global agriculture

In exploring these examples of global capitalism, we have rather neglected agriculture. Arguably, global agriculture is nothing new and has long flourished in the tea plantations of India and Sri Lanka or the fruit plantations of Central America. The international division of labour established in the 19th century created new markets in the industrial societies for the agricultural products of the rest of the world and Western corporations invested capital in their large-scale production.

8. Large-scale banana production by Dole in Ecuador.

In agriculture too, however, there has been growing international competition and capitalist production has spread. In the 1990s there was a crisis in the banana industry, which was producing more bananas than the market could absorb. American fruit corporations, notably Dole, began to shift production to Ecuador, where wages and other labour costs were substantially lower and there were no labour unions (Figure 8). Unions of banana workers were subsequently created but have faced frequent and violent attacks. The banana companies also used the World Trade Organization (WTO) to pressurize the European Union (EU) to end its preferential treatment of the banana growers in the ex-colonial territories of Africa and the Caribbean, where bananas were grown largely by small farmers with higher costs, who in a free market could not hope to compete successfully with the corporations. Eventually in 2010 the EU reduced its preferential treatment of the small producer countries, while providing financial support to help them 'adjust to new trade realities over the next few years'.

Small producers have also found themselves driven in other ways towards capitalist agriculture. Vandana Shiva has argued that agriculture is becoming increasingly dominated by highly concentrated 'life science corporations', which cut across agribusiness, biotechnology, and the chemical and pharmaceutical industries. These corporations sell genetically engineered seed, which can produce large crops and, it is claimed, cure deficiency diseases, through, for example, adding vitamin A to rice. This kind of agriculture can be very productive of cash crops but it requires the extensive use of the pesticides and herbicides also sold by these corporations, and large amounts of water. The environmental consequences can be disastrous, as scarce water resources are used up, chemical pollution increases, and biodiversity is lost. Farmers not only become dependent on the corporations but also go into debt, since considerable investment is required, and can then end up losing their land if poor harvests or other disasters destroy their capacity to service their debts.

Small-scale agriculture loses its viability and large capital intensive units take over.

Allied to this process is a commodification of nature, as plants, seeds, genes, and water, which were previously natural resources, often available freely to all, become commodities that have a monetary value. Knowledge itself has become commodified. The WTO's Trade Related Intellectual Property Rights Agreement requires countries to allow the patenting of information about plant strains and genetic material. Vandana Shiva argues that this means:

> The knowledge of the poor is being converted into the property of global corporations, creating a situation where the poor will have to pay for the seeds and medicines they have evolved and have used to meet their own needs for nutrition and health care.

Global money

The spread of the capitalist practices that we have been examining inevitably generated an increasing circulation of money, but the truly astonishing rise in its international circulation during the last quarter of the 20th century was mainly the result of speculative money movements. International investment, most of which was speculative in character, increased by a factor of nearly 200 between 1970 and 1997, according to Manuel Castells. By the end of the century global currency trading amounted to $1.5 *trillion a day* but it did not stop there and in 2011 had reached $5 trillion a day. This huge increase was not to do with currency trading to enable foreign travel or international trade, though this clearly happened, but was speculation to make money out of currency movements.

Technical advances made possible this expansion of international currency dealing and investment. This was partly to do with communications, for geo-stationary satellites, the digital transmission of data, and computer networks increased both the speed of transactions and the sheer amount of business that could be handled. It was also a matter of financial technology and innovation; many new ways of investing in the markets and channelling capital into them were created by a flourishing financial services industry.

The now infamous 'derivatives', of the kind traded so disastrously by Nick Leeson (see Chapter 1), were the most sophisticated new financial instruments. Money was also more straightforwardly channelled through investment funds into the 'emerging markets' that began to attract investment in the 1980s. There were opportunities here for investors to buy cheaply into newly industrializing countries and then realize gains when prices rose. The financial industries of the affluent societies rapidly created a whole range of such funds to tap into the savings of ordinary people.

The floating of currencies in the 1970s had created new uncertainties and new opportunities, which stimulated currency trading and futures markets. 'Floating' meant that currency values were determined not by official rates but by the market, rising and falling according to the supply of a currency and the demand for it. There was greater uncertainty for companies that needed foreign currencies for their operations and they therefore needed to protect themselves by trading in futures. Above all, however, currency trading increased because of the greater opportunities that floating rates provided for speculation.

Why had currencies been floated in this way? Previously, under the system set up at the Bretton Woods conference of 1944, currency values had been fixed in relation to the dollar, which in turn had its value fixed in relation to gold. The stability this provided enabled the expansion of international trade and a period of steady economic growth. In the early 1970s, however, it proved more and more difficult to maintain the fixed value of the dollar and the United States government was forced to devalue it. There were particular reasons for the devaluation of the dollar at this time, notably the consequences of government spending on the Vietnam War, but the Bretton Woods system had anyway come under a growing strain.

This was because fixed official exchange rates could only be maintained if governments either pursued unpopular policies or controlled the movement of money across their borders. If a growing trade deficit put pressure on the existing rate, and speculators began to bet on a devaluation, governments could act to maintain the value of their currency. They could, for example, reduce consumption in order to curb imports but this was politically very difficult in democratic societies. Alternatively, they could try to stop speculators moving money around through exchange controls. But it became harder to control money movements in this way as trade increased, as holdings of some countries' currencies, above all the US dollar, accumulated abroad, and as larger amounts of money began to move between countries.

The deregulatory spirit of the remarketized capitalism of the 1980s, which we examined in Chapter 3, also played its part in all this. Exchange rates fixed by the state and controls on the international movement of money did not accord with the renewed belief in free markets and competition.

Nor did they accord with the growth of financial industries and increasing competition between them, for the health of these industries depended on their capacity to draw an international flow of money through their markets. Competition between the established financial centres of the world lay behind the City of London's 'big bang' deregulation in October 1987, as London tried to catch up with New York. Competition was also coming from new financial centres, and by the 1990s there were some thirty-five stock markets in developing countries. Some have become highly sophisticated financial centres, and it was through dealing on the

Simex financial futures exchange in Singapore that Nick Leeson made and lost his reputation.

There has been a quite remarkable growth in the global flow of money. Advances in communications technology made this possible but it was driven by the growth of financial industries, increasing international competition, and the remarketizing of capitalism.

How global is global?

Capitalist institutions and practices have been spreading across the world, but at this point we must halt a moment and consider quite how global 'global capitalism' really is.

The circulation of money across the world has increased but is it circulating globally? Even though new countries were industrializing, new financial centres had emerged in developing countries, and investment in 'emerging markets' had become fashionable, most of the money still flowed between the already developed societies.

Thus, although the foreign investment going into poor countries has increased, rich countries still receive disproportionate amounts of this, while the investment that does go into poor countries remains heavily concentrated in particular areas. According to UNCTAD, around half of foreign investment still goes into developed countries. Around a quarter goes into East Asia, mainly into China, though other countries such as Indonesia, Malaysia, and Singapore are catching up. Other parts of Asia, including India, and Africa receive very little. In 2011 the whole of Africa received under 3 per cent of total foreign investment. Investment is not globally spread.

Some have thought that globalization would result in equalization, as poor countries eventually caught up with rich ones. Japan, which became for a time the world's second largest economy, showed that this could happen. China, which has displaced Japan to become second in the world (though this is less impressive than it might appear to be, given its huge population), and some other Asian economies have also shown this is possible. Will international differences be eliminated as a global capitalist economy becomes established?

The claim that globalization equalizes has been viewed with considerable scepticism by Robert Wade, who points out that it is largely dependent on the Chinese case. What about the rest of the world? Furthermore, Amartya Sen has argued forcefully that the differences between rich and poor countries are so huge that marginal changes in international inequality are of no real significance.

Should one anyway focus on *international* inequality? Thomas Piketty has examined the distribution of global wealth. For him the key point is that the returns earned on capital, especially the capital owned by the richest people, have been higher than the growth of average global incomes during the years 1987–2013, which means that inequalities of wealth have increased. This comes out particularly forcefully when the wealth of the richest is considered. According to Forbes data, cited by Piketty, while dollar billionaires owned 0.4 per cent of global private wealth in 1987, they owned more than 1.5 per cent in 2013. The number of billionaires rose from 5 per 100 million adults in 1987 to 30 per million in 2013. Arguably, what matters is not so much international inequality as such but growing disparities of wealth. In a future world of probably low economic growth, these disparities can only increase.

Another problem with 'globalization' is the implication that a new level of global organization has emerged that transcends national units, as with the term 'global corporation'. There are certainly many transnational corporations, in the sense that corporations operate in different countries and across national boundaries, but most operate in only a few countries and are hardly global in character.

They are often seen as flouting the nation-state, particularly by transferring employment abroad, but all are based in a nation-state somewhere and most actually have the bulk of their assets and provide most of their employment in this state. They exploit the facilities of their home nation-state, its infrastructure and institutions, and use its power to promote and assist their operations abroad. They may provide employment in poor countries, but they also exploit their cheap labour, drive out local competitors, and channel profits back to their home state. As Peter Dicken has argued, transnational corporations are also national corporations, and most cannot really be described as global at all.

Capitalism is global in the sense that it reaches almost everywhere but in a very uneven way. The flow of money and investment is so unevenly spread across the globe that it is in some ways misleading to describe it as 'global'. Commonly used terms, such as 'global capitalism' and 'global economy' gloss over huge inequalities, and the continuing importance of national units and national governments.

Global capitalist dominance

In one respect there can, however, be little doubt that capitalism has gone global and that is in the elimination of alternative systems.

The year 1989 saw the main global alternative, state socialism, begin to collapse. Gorbachev initiated a regime of 'restructuring and openness' in the Soviet Union, which also began to loosen its grip on its East European satellites. The Soviet economy had operated on the basis of central planning and the bureaucratic direction of the economy, with markets operating only at the margins. It has been castigated and ridiculed for its inefficiency, its low productivity, its poor overall economic performance, and pollution of the environment, which all apparently made it living proof of the superiority of capitalism. Its record of industrialization and substantial economic growth, its maintenance of full employment and low inflation, and its capable provision of education and health care have now been largely forgotten, though no doubt many Russians still remember the stability and security it once provided.

It collapsed largely because it could not compete with the more dynamic capitalist economies of the West. Expectations had been rising in Russia and Eastern Europe, for in a world of growing communication, people could not be insulated from the individualist consumer culture of the West. Economies operating under the constraints of state socialism could not meet these expectations, or at least not while so much of their resources was devoted to military production. It was arguably the burden imposed by the Cold War that was insupportable, and Reagan's 'Star Wars' programme may well have been the final blow, since it sharply escalated the military-industrial competition between the superpowers.

Gorbachev had tried to introduce a programme of gradual reform, but no gradual transition from a command to a market economy occurred. Once state direction ceased, economic paralysis followed, and under Yeltsin an attempt was made to jolt Russia into capitalism. The 'shock therapy' administered to the economy in 1991 freed prices from state control and by the end of 1994 had privatized three-quarters of Russia's medium and large enterprises. The consequences were catastrophic for most ordinary people. According to John Gray's account, between 1991 and 1996 consumer prices increased by a factor of 1,700 and some 45 million people fell into poverty.

While the collapse of state socialism removed the main alternative model, developing societies were forced by financial pressures and international institutions to conform to the dominant American model of capitalism. A key role in this was played by American-dominated international financial institutions—the World Bank and the International Monetary Fund (IMF). Both were created during the Second World War by the same Bretton Woods conference that set up the postwar system of fixed exchange rates. The World Bank was to assist countries with postwar reconstruction and development, while the IMF was charged with maintaining international economic stability. Although their functions were different, in the 1980s these institutions began to jointly promote the free-market ideologies and policies that increasingly held sway in the United States and other leading industrial societies. Like other international institutions, they were dominated by their most powerful members.

They advocated three key and interrelated policies. The first of these was fiscal austerity to reduce wasteful government spending and eliminate loose monetary policies leading to inflation. The second was privatization to get rid of inefficient public enterprises, introduce market discipline, and also reduce government spending. The third was liberalization, the removal of barriers to trade, with the assistance of the 1995-founded World Trade Organization, and the ending of government interference with the operation of markets. These policies were implemented through 'conditionality'. The loans made by these bodies were conditional on the pursuit of such policies. The high dependence of developing societies on loans meant that they were in a very weak position to resist such policies, however inappropriate they might be. Indeed, these policies were implemented in developing countries more rigorously than they were in the developed societies themselves. The United States, Europe, and Japan have all heavily protected and subsidized their agriculture.

Joseph Stiglitz, a senior figure at the World Bank between 1997 and 2000, has written a scathing critique of these policies, particularly as implemented by the IMF. He was not opposed to the policies themselves, which could bring benefits in some circumstances, but to their indiscriminate and over-hasty imposition. In inappropriate situations austerity could destroy valuable projects dependent on government expenditure and create mass unemployment, while privatization could lead to the plundering of public assets and higher prices for consumers. As for liberalization, particularly of financial markets, this could simply open the door to an invasion by foreign capital. Indeed, Stiglitz suggests that the IMF's policies in this regard were often driven by its links with Wall Street financial interests.

The policies were implemented as though there were no alternatives. Stiglitz draws a contrast between the experience of Russia and the experience of China. IMF advice led Russia into 'shock therapy' and the creation of mass poverty, while China's opposite strategy of gradualist transition 'entailed the largest reduction in poverty in history in such a short time span'. The secret of China's success was that instead of destroying old institutions China allowed new capitalist enterprises to develop within the existing social order. It did not make the mistake of mass privatization but rather created the conditions within which a private sector could emerge and flourish, following, as it happens, the advice given by Stiglitz!

This was not, of course, just a matter of choosing the right policies and policy advisers, for China's more effective elite, with a stronger economy and state, were in a much better position than the paralysed rulers of a disintegrating Soviet Union to go their own way towards capitalism and control the transition. Shocks and conflicts may, anyway, lie ahead for the Chinese model, which appears to be making a successful economic transition from communism to capitalism, but may also be creating a dislocated proletariat with few channels for the expression of discontent, in the absence of a political transition.

The state socialist alternative has collapsed and, as the only viable economic system, capitalism has become globally dominant.

There can be no doubt that capitalism has delivered goods and services in much greater quantities and with far greater choice than state socialism ever did. This does not, however, mean that there is only one route to economic success, for there are different routes to capitalism and, as we saw in the last chapter, different ways of organizing it. We should not confuse the elimination of alternatives *to* capitalism with the elimination of alternatives *within* it.

The myths of global capitalism

'Global capitalism' is a short-hand phrase that conveys the idea that in recent years the institutions and practices of capitalism have spread into new areas of the world and connected distant parts closely together in new ways. There can be no doubt that this has happened and that there has consequently been a profound transformation of the world in which we live. Capitalism is the globally dominant system and will continue to be so in the foreseeable future.

In the course of this chapter, we have, however, found that the notion of global capitalism has also generated powerful and misleading myths. *Myth one* is that global capitalism is recent, for it has deep historical roots. *Myth two* is that capital circulates globally, when in reality most of it moves between a small group of rich countries. *Myth three* is that capitalism is now organized globally rather than nationally, for international differences are as important as ever and nation-states continue to play a key role in the activities of transnational corporations. *Myth four* is that global capitalism integrates the world, since the more global capitalism has become, the more divided the world has become by inequalities of wealth.

Chapter 6
Crisis? What crisis?

Those living in the midst of an economic crisis may well feel that their world is collapsing. They may indeed think that the whole capitalist system is coming to an end. Crises of capitalism are not, however, exceptional events but rather a normal part of the functioning of a capitalist society. In the 19th century they became a regular feature of economic life, though crisis mechanisms that are familiar in today's world actually appeared centuries earlier. This chapter begins with the 'tulipomania' of 17th-century Holland, which shows the same basic mechanisms in operation as recent stock-market bubbles.

The tulip bubble in 17th-century Amsterdam

After their 16th-century arrival from Turkey, tulips, especially the more exotic and rarer specimens, had become highly prized in 17th-century Holland. Tulip growing spread in its rich alluvial soil but scarce supply and high demand resulted in rapidly rising prices. Its high profitability attracted many into this trade, where little investment was required and money could easily be made.

The high demand for bulbs led to rapid changes in the bulb trade. At first bulbs were sold in large quantities, sometimes in complete beds, but as demand grew these were broken down into smaller units until individual bulbs, particularly those of the most valuable varieties, were traded. Then a market developed in the outgrowths from the bulb, the clones from which future bulbs could be grown. Finally, in the 1630s, the tulip trade generated the market in tulip futures that led to the 'tulipomania' of 1636–7.

How did this happen? Initially, the trading season was short and lasted only a few months after the flowering and lifting of the bulbs. To meet expanding demand traders began buying and selling tulips that were still in the ground. They were now in effect buying and selling bulb futures. Promissory notes specified the details of the tulip bought and when it would be lifted, while a sign in the ground identified the owner. It was then but a small step to trade in the notes rather than the bulbs, for rapidly rising bulb prices gave the notes themselves an increasing value.

The tulip futures trade became a wildly speculative bubble, where prices were pushed up not by the demand for bulbs but the demand for the 'paper' futures. Since only a deposit had to be made on the future purchase, a small amount of money went a long way, so long as the contract note could be unloaded on someone else at a profit before full payment became due. As contract dates approached, dealing became increasingly frenzied and the notes circulated faster. Prices eventually rose to the point at which no-one was prepared to buy and then suddenly collapsed. There was no real demand for many of the quite ordinary tulips that had been drawn into the speculative dealing at the height of the boom. Since no-one actually wanted these bulbs, the right to buy them in the future was ultimately worthless and there was, therefore, no floor to the crashing market.

Trading in futures was the central mechanism in the inflation of this bubble and at this time was already an established practice of merchant capitalism but it was, interestingly, not the merchants who were the main players. Some did become involved but the really big merchants, who were busy making relatively risk-free money from their monopolies, seem to have held aloof. The bubble was inflated as ordinary people, such as weavers, bricklayers, carpenters, and cobblers, became involved. They raised capital by using up their savings, borrowing, mortgaging their property, or making payments in kind. Simon Schama gives the example of the purchase of just one rare bulb with 'two *last* of wheat and four of rye, four fat oxen, eight pigs, a dozen sheep, two oxheads of wine, four tons of butter, a thousand pounds of cheese, a bed, some clothing and a silver beaker'.

The trading of bulbs and notes was not carried out in the Amsterdam stock exchange, though there was plenty of other speculative activity going on there, but in the taverns where 'colleges' of traders met and drank. These colleges developed their own secret procedures, trading rituals, and festivities, a poor man's version of those at the stock exchange. Speculative capitalism was then, as it is now, not just the province of sophisticated financiers.

Crises of the 19th century

Serious as its consequences were for those involved, the bursting of the tulip bubble did not impact significantly on the economy as a whole. There was not at this time a sufficiently high integration of economic activities to spread a crisis in one area to the whole economy. It was the growth of capitalist production that produced the necessary linkages to make crises economy-wide. Furthermore, capitalist production actually generated new crisis mechanisms, which Karl Marx analysed.

Marx argued that capitalism was prone to crises because production was separated from consumption. In pre-capitalist societies they were closely related, since most production was for more or less immediate consumption. Under capitalism, goods were increasingly produced for sale in markets and this relationship became more distant. Goods were produced in the expectation that they could be sold, but the market might be unable to absorb them. Marx described capitalism as anarchic because production was no longer directly regulated by the needs of those consuming its products.

A tendency to overproduce was in fact built into capitalist production. Competition between producers generated a pressure to expand production, since higher volume reduced costs, cheapened prices, and enlarged market share. When the amount of goods produced exceeded the demand for them, there would be an overproduction crisis and prices would fall, eventually below the level at which profits could be made. This not only damaged the industry concerned but had knock-on effects that spread the crisis. Investment would decline and hit those industries producing machinery. Workers would be laid off or wages lowered, which would further reduce consumer demand. In these ways, overproduction generated vicious circles, leading to closures and bankruptcies, and high levels of unemployment.

Mass unemployment then resulted in a social crisis, for in a capitalist economy people were in a quite new way dependent on wage labour for their survival. Such crises occurred roughly every ten years during the first half of the 19th century.

Although unemployment caused great suffering and some capitalists went out of business, these crises did not destroy capitalism. Indeed, Marx argued that it was crises that made it possible for capitalism to continue, since they eliminated the strains of overproduction, forced out the least efficient producers, and enabled the renewed operation of virtuous circles, once closures and bankruptcies had reduced production to a level closer to demand. Similarly, lower wages increased profitability and cheaper prices stimulated demand. Lower interest rates made it cheaper to borrow money for investment. Production could start to expand again, employment would rise, and there would be more people with money in their pockets to buy goods.

Capitalism would therefore expand its way out of crisis but, he argued in the *Communist Manifesto,* this expansion would only lead to 'more extensive and more destructive crises'. This did not mean that Marx believed that capitalism would be ended by some huge economic collapse. It would come to an end only when overthrown by the workers it exploited. Certain tendencies in its development would, however, facilitate this eventual overthrow. The advance of technology and the concentration of ownership would increase the size of units of production, concentrating workers in larger masses that would be easier to organize. Crises would certainly play a part in all this by radicalizing workers through their experience of them. They would also be radicalized by the widening gulf between the wealth of the increasingly small group of capitalists who enjoyed the profits of capital and the poverty of the masses.

Ownership did become more concentrated, units of production increased in size, and workers became more organized, but Marx's expectation that the working class would become increasingly radical and ultimately revolutionary has not been borne out. Workers were coerced into an acceptance of capitalism by their economic dependence on employment and the repression of revolutionary movements that sought to overthrow the capitalist system. They have been incorporated through their organizations into the political structures of capitalist societies, and seduced by the flood of goods and services that capitalist production has provided. There was, anyway, no crisis of a sufficient scale to threaten the capitalist economic system until the 1930s.

The Great Depression in the 1930s

A period of reasonably steady growth, if not without crises, lasted from the middle of the 19th century until the First World War and this apparently resumed in the 1920s but the ending of the war left the world economy in a fragile state. The City of London's stabilizing financial dominance had now passed into history and international economic relationships were disorganized and unstable during the 1920s. Furthermore, the war and its aftermath had left many countries, above all Germany, heavily in debt and with weakened economies that made it difficult to service and repay debts. This was the background to the Great Depression of the 1930s, a depression so deep and extensive that Eric Hobsbawm considers it 'amounted to something very close to the collapse of the capitalist world economy'.

It was the 1929 collapse of the Wall Street stock market in New York that signalled the plunge into depression. New York prices crashed in October 1929 but then continued downwards until they hit bottom in June 1932, having lost over 80 per cent of their value since their September 1929 peak.

Cumulative mechanisms depressed the economy. Production declined throughout the industrial world and this resulted in sharply rising unemployment, which reduced demand and led to the further contraction of production. In the United States, industrial production fell by one-third during the years 1929–31 and over a quarter of the labour force was unemployed at the bottom of the slump. Work prospects became so dire that people would auction their labour to the highest bidder (see Figure 9). Unemployed workers could no longer pay the interest on their house loans and this threatened the solvency of local banks. They could no longer afford to buy consumer goods, especially cars, and American car production halved, throwing more people out of work. Low state benefits at this time not only made unemployment a far worse experience than it is in today's industrial societies, they also meant that mass unemployment could eliminate the purchasing power of a large part of the population.

There was also a severe depression in agriculture. As consumer demand declined and stocks accumulated, the prices of agricultural products fell, tea and wheat prices dropping by

9. Labour is auctioned to the highest bidder during the 1930s Depression in the United States.

two-thirds and the price of silk by three-quarters. Farmers reacted by increasing production in a vain attempt to maintain their incomes but this led to prices falling even further. The dominant images of the 1930s are of the unemployed in Europe and America lining up at soup kitchens or setting off on hunger marches. Countries such as Argentina, Brazil, and Cuba, or Australia and New Zealand, with economies dependent on their export of food and raw materials to the industrial societies, were equally devastated.

The 1930s demonstrated the capitalist world economy's *vulnerability* to crisis. The problem was not so much the occurrence of crisis, for, as we have seen, crises are part of the normal machinery of capitalism, but the ensuing crash of capitalist economies across the world, as cumulative mechanisms spread and deepened the crisis. Three main sources of this vulnerability can be identified.

There was first the huge growth in productive capacity that had taken place over the previous century. This meant that equally huge levels of demand were necessary if production was to be absorbed and applied not only to the production of manufactured goods but also to food and other primary products. Insufficient demand has been interpreted not only as overproduction but also as under-consumption by poorly paid workers. Either way, the increasing scale of production and the growing numbers of people employed in it meant that a failure of consumption to keep pace with production could precipitate a rapid downward spiral of the economy, as workers, who were also consumers, lost their jobs.

The second was the international division of labour that integrated the world economy. The industrial societies produced the manufactured goods and the rest of the world concentrated on producing food and raw materials. If demand fell in the industrial societies, the primary producers exporting, say, beef, coffee, or sugar, to them found that their sales, prices, and incomes dropped. When their incomes dropped, the overseas markets for industrial goods declined. Some historians consider the depression began in the primary producer countries and was then transmitted to the industrial societies, while others have argued the opposite, but, either way, a crisis in one group of countries was inevitably transmitted to the other and then reverberated between them. Global economic integration was another mechanism that amplified the depression.

The third was the tension between international trade and national protection. As the first industrial nation, Britain had promoted free-trade policies, which maximized the markets for its products. When other countries industrialized, they were inevitably more protectionist, since their infant industries needed protection in order to establish themselves. A growing international competition then generated ever more calls for national protection. British economic dominance and global economic growth had none the less maintained free trade until the First World War, but after this war, and partly because of it, the international economy was no longer dominated by Britain and no longer characterized by stable economic growth.

When domestic production faced a crisis, it was hard to resist the temptation to protect the national economy against foreign competition and as soon as action of this kind was taken by one country, others followed. In particular, the introduction of extensive tariff protection of its economy by the United States in 1930 triggered a retaliation by other countries. Furthermore, the 19th-century division of the world between competing empires provided the industrial societies both with an illusion of self-sufficiency and ready-made structures within which they could shelter. The result was a cumulative decline of world trade that made the depression worse.

Out of the depression emerged a new set of policies designed to prevent it ever happening again. Governments were accustomed to respond to depression by cutting their expenditure or raising taxes, in order to balance their books when declining economic activity reduced their tax revenue. John Maynard Keynes argued that such policies just made things worse. Governments could counteract tendencies towards depression by injecting demand into the economy, by borrowing and spending or by lowering taxes. These 'Keynesian' policies began to make an impact in some countries in the later 1930s, though it was above all the huge state expenditure generated by the Second World War that hauled the global economy out of the depression.

From postwar boom to new crisis

During the quarter-century after the end of the Second World War it really did seem as though the crisis tendencies of capitalism had been overcome. Governments thought they now knew how to use Keynesian policies to prevent crises getting out of control. Heavy government spending had not stopped, for the United

States was now engaged in a new war, the Cold War with the Soviet Union. This led not only to military expenditure overseas but also to the deliberate revival of the Japanese and European economies, since these areas were in the front line of the Cold War. It also led to the space race, as the United States reacted to Soviet success in putting Gagarin into space by pouring money into its own space programme. This was an expansive dynamism that was very different from the isolationist protectionism of the interwar period. The largest economy in the world was spreading economic growth across it.

Technological advance greatly increased production but an overproduction crisis was avoided because consumer demand too was steadily increasing. Higher productivity meant that the prices of goods came down, so that they fell increasingly within the reach of the workers who made them. Car ownership, for example, was spreading down the social scale. Greater productivity also allowed workers' wages to rise, while full employment maximized worker bargaining power.

It should be said that much of this growth was at others' expense. The affluence of the industrial societies depended on the low prices of the primary products from the rest of the world. The low price of oil was particularly crucial, because it was not only a fuel but also the basis of a wide range of synthetic materials. These were substituted for the 'natural' products of the Third World and further drove down the prices they could command. Thus, synthetic textiles diminished the demand for cotton. The relationship between the prices of manufactured goods and primary products changed to the disadvantage of the primary producers, who found that by 1970 manufactured goods were costing them one-third more than they had done in 1951.

In the 1970s all this changed, for the 'virtuous' circles, if they can be described as such, that had enabled the growth of the two previous decades turned 'vicious' as the international economy hit the buffers. A rise in the prices of many primary products, notably oil, steadily increased industrial costs and shop prices, both hitting profits and diminishing real wages and, therefore, reducing spending power. Profits were hit not only by these rising costs but also by wage increases, as workers reacted to price rises by demanding higher pay to maintain their standard of living. The continued growth of trade unions gave them the muscle to do this.

This was a crisis quite different in character to that of the 1930s. In the 1930s demand had collapsed but now there was too much demand, which forced prices and wages up. Furthermore, the floating of currencies after the collapse of fixed exchange rates relaxed monetary controls on inflation, for governments were now under less pressure to guard the value of their currency in order to maintain these rates.

Increasing international competition intensified the crisis. The recovery of Germany and Japan from the destruction wrought on their economies by defeat in the Second World War brought modern and highly efficient industries into production. This further increased the pressure on world resources and also generated a new overproduction crisis.

The impact of Japan on the profitability of the industries of the old industrial societies was particularly devastating, because in Japan government and industry cooperated very effectively in pursuing long-term policies designed to create new industries and capture markets, while Japanese productivity was much higher. It was the old industrial societies that faced particular problems in dealing with this crisis. Their development of managed capitalism had, as we saw in Chapter 3, restricted or replaced the market mechanisms that would have promoted a rapid rationalizing response. An effective response had to wait upon the remarketizing of their economies by the governments of the 1980s.

Growing instability

After the 1970s a new world of slower growth and greater instability emerged. Growth rates in the last quarter of the 20th century were half those of the previous quarter. Many countries were on the edge of crisis much of the time, while globalization meant that crises could move easily from one country to another.

This was a world of spreading industry and intensified international competition. As we have seen, the growth of international competition was one of the processes that had already led to lower profitability in the old industrial societies during the 1970s. Lower profitability then resulted in companies seeking to restore profits by finding cheaper labour in other countries, spreading industrial employment to new areas of the world, notably to East and South-East Asia. The industrialization of China began to bring another quarter of the world's population into the capitalist world economy. All this increased international competition still further.

Higher production, resulting from increased capacity and technological change, could be absorbed if demand increased as well, but global demand did not expand at the same rate as the supply of goods. After all, one reason why new centres of production emerged was the availability of cheap labour, and low wages did not generate much consumer demand. Consumer demand in the developed countries too was faltering. Companies reduced wage costs in order to at least try to compete with cheap imports from the new industrializers. The continuing deindustrialization of the old industrial societies meant that labour was shifted from 'good jobs' in manufacturing to poorly paid service work. Privatization exposed cushioned state employees to the rigours of the open labour market. Higher unemployment depressed consumer demand. How could the flood of products from the Far East be absorbed?

Consumption was maintained by increasing debt. Hire purchase had long existed as a means of borrowing to finance the consumption of particularly expensive goods, notably cars, but the invention and multiplication of credit cards turned borrowing into the *normal* means of paying for all goods and services. The buying of houses through mortgage borrowing became a normal means by which people acquired somewhere to live, though mortgages could also be used to finance the purchase of all sorts of other things. The deregulation of financial services by the 'big bang' of the 1990s stimulated a competitive lending by banks (and building societies) which further generated the growth of debt.

Indeed, in the United States in the 1990s householders were encouraged to take out 'second mortgages' to finance general consumption. This was, according to Raguram Rajan, a response to the growing inequality of income there. Governments were unable to please the electorate by increasing the incomes of those falling behind, so they compensated them by providing easy credit that enabled a higher level of consumption. They spurred on lending agencies to encourage people to take out second mortgages and kept interest-rates low.

The flow of money to the consumer countries of the West from the producer countries of the East, which had to do something with the money their exports were earning, also helped to keep interest-rates low. In this way the gap between production and consumption could be bridged at least for the time being but at the cost of rising levels of debt, which were a further source of economic instability.

While one response of the owners of capital to the declining profitability of production was to search for cheaper labour abroad, another was, as Giovanni Arrighi has argued, to shift capital from investment in production to investment in shares, currencies, and derivatives. The owners of capital could more easily make money through speculative trading in these financial instruments than through struggling to make it from the production of goods and services in a tough and uncertain economic environment.

There were certainly now massive new opportunities to make money in this way. As outlined in the section 'Global money' (see Chapter 5), the floating of exchange rates and the removal of national barriers to the movement of money, together with financial deregulation, opened the way to speculative activities. During the period since 1980, there was a huge flow of money into financial activities, a process labelled the 'financialization of capital'. One indication of this is the growth in the economic weight of the banks. Back in 1960 the balance-sheets of the British clearing banks comprised £8 billion, some 38 per cent of Gross Domestic Product, but in 2010 they had reached £6.4 *trillion*, an astonishing 450 per cent of GDP. Thus, the banks' balance-sheets were by then between four and five times the size of the productive economy. What Michael Hudson has termed 'balance-sheet wealth' was supplanting the creation of wealth through productive investment.

Increasing international competition, the growth of debt, deregulation, and the financialization of capital had produced a cocktail of destabilizing forces. These led to the crisis that started in 2007.

The 2007–8 crisis and the 'great recession'

The immediate origins of the crisis lay in a house market bubble in the United States, which also occurred in many other countries, including Britain. Prices seemed to rise endlessly, making houses an apparently safe investment, both for those buying and those lending them the money. Banks competed aggressively to lend, with commission payments and bonuses spurring their salespeople on. One practice common in the US was to lure in borrowers by offering loans at initially very low rates of interest. Loans were also increasingly made to so-called 'sub-prime' borrowers with poor credit ratings. This frenzy of lending occurred not just because money could be made from the mortgage business but because the lenders could 'securitize' the loans, packaging them up and selling them on to other financial institutions looking for apparently safe and profitable ways to invest their money. Financial engineering had turned loans on houses into financial products that could be bought and sold.

House prices could not go on rising for ever and it was hardly surprising that the house market bubble eventually burst. Few, however, expected that this would lead to a full-blown crisis of capitalism. Why did this happen?

Many 'sub-prime' borrowers had been persuaded to take loans they could not afford to service, with a view to sell on their property as prices rose. When house prices began to fall, the financial institutions which had made the loans or bought them as investments could not get their money back. But what really turned this situation into a crisis was the heavy indebtedness of these institutions. They had themselves borrowed vast amounts of money, often from abroad, to make the loans or buy the securitized loan packages. Lehman Brothers, the US investment bank, had debts that amounted to over forty times its capital.

The banks had made good profits from this 'leverage' and their share prices had risen, but they did not realize how dangerous their situation was. They thought they were safe, because they had used sophisticated new financial techniques that were supposed to eliminate the risk of default. These techniques were, however, poorly understood by senior managers and promised far more than they could deliver. Apparently rock-solid US financial institutions—the New York investment banks Bear Stearns, Merrill Lynch, and Lehmann Brothers; the mortgage finance corporations Fanny Mae and Freddie Mac; and the global insurance giant AIG—had hugely overextended themselves and faced bankruptcy.

The crisis then spread. One big name after another had to be rescued by governments but, after Lehmann Brothers in the US was allowed to go bankrupt in September 2008, there was a global financial panic. Was any bank anywhere safe? Banks fearing that loans might not be repaid became very reluctant to lend to each other in the normal way, and interest-rates on loans between them rose. Those with huge debts tried desperately to rebuild their capital. Capital was now being hoarded.

This was no longer just a crisis for the banks. It spread through the whole economy because the hoarding of capital froze the financial system. Normal economic activity is lubricated by the movement of money between those with money to lend and those needing finance but a 'credit crunch' ground this movement to a halt. Ordinary companies needing to borrow to finance their daily activities found that loans had suddenly become very hard to obtain. Governments tried desperately to get interest-rates down and banks lending again.

The financial freeze then set off the cumulative deflationary processes of the 'great recession'. Bankruptcies, rising unemployment and falling wages, falling sales and prices, interacted to depress economic activity. Fearful of the future, people started to save more and spend less, depressing demand. Producers drew in their horns and investment ground to a halt. A repeat of the Great Depression of the 1930s beckoned. Although the giant economies of China and India were still growing, albeit more slowly, there were fears that deflation might go global.

Yet another stage in the crisis now developed. At the very time when they needed to spend more in order to deal with the consequences of the crisis, governments found that their tax revenue was falling. Banks that had been lending large sums of money to governments worried that these might not be able to service, let alone repay their debts, and might default. Governments in a weak financial position found themselves downgraded by the agencies that assessed credit-worthiness, which meant that the banks lending to them imposed higher interest-rates on their loans, to cover their greater risk, thereby making governments' fiscal position even worse.

This was a vicious circle that plunged first Greece and then other European countries, notably Ireland, Portugal, and Spain, into desperate expenditure cuts, which in turn deepened the downward deflationary spiral of their economies. Their situation was worsened by their membership of the Eurozone, which severely restricted their freedom of action and prevented them using currency devaluation to ease their economic problems. But this was not only a problem for financially weak Eurozone states. In the fraught post-crisis climate of opinion, governments in general worried about their debts and deficits, and feared that they might succumb to the same process unless they cut state expenditure.

Are we recovering?

This had been the most serious crisis since the 1930s. How did governments respond? Is the world recovering?

The severity of the crisis elicited a strong response from governments, which feared a complete collapse of the banking system and a prolonged depression. In the UK this response most immediately took the form of nationalizing the failing banks. As early as February 2008 the British Northern Rock bank, which had been rashly lending up to 125 per cent of a property's value, was nationalized after its share price collapsed. The Royal Bank of Scotland (RBS), which had expanded aggressively to become one of the biggest banks in the world, came within days of bankruptcy in October 2008 and after successive state injections of capital was by February 2009 84 per cent state-owned. It should not be supposed, however, that this marked a reversal of the process of remarketizing capitalism, for these nationalizations were temporary. By January 2012 Northern Rock had been sold to Virgin Money. It is expected that RBS will be re-privatized in a few years' time.

There have been many calls for reforms that would prevent such a crisis occurring again. If banks have become 'too big to fail', should they not be broken up? The 1980/90s ending of the historic separation of retail from investment banking has been widely seen as one of the main causes of the financial crisis. Should not these functions be once again divorced? The debate on these issues goes on and some politicians have taken up strong positions but so far very little has actually happened on either front. Financial businesses resist regulation and any attempt to do this comes up against the argument that banks can easily move to another country, taking jobs and tax revenue with them. International competition to attract/retain their business makes effective regulation virtually impossible.

As Geoffrey Ingham has put it:

> Whatever the eventual scope of any re-regulation of banking and financial asset trading, history suggests that it will have little long-term effect. From its position at the apex of capitalist power, finance-capital has proved to be adept at evading control and at developing new financial instruments and practices that are not covered by existing regulations, as occurred in the incubation of the current crisis.

And, one might add, this has already been happening with the growth of the ultra-fast and high-frequency computer-driven trading that has reportedly come to account for the bulk of Wall Street transactions. In May 2010 a computer malfunction resulted in a blizzard of trades, causing a 'flash crash', though one that was contained. 'Kill switches' and 'circuit-breakers' are supposed to prevent such a crash becoming a disaster.

The regulation of banking could not, anyway, deal with the 'great recession'. Indeed, banks' attempts, under government pressure, to build up larger capital reserves made them less able to resume the normal lending activities that the economy required. Central banks tried to get normal economic activity going again by lowering interest-rates and by printing money through a process known as 'quantitative easing' (QE). This has assisted a recovery to take place, at least in Britain and the United States, but whether it has laid the ghost of deflation is another matter.

In 2014 many economies, particularly in the European Union, were close to deflation or actually experiencing it. Once deflationary processes have started it can be very hard to extricate an economy from them, as the Japanese case described in Chapter 4 has shown. There have been fears that a global deflation might set in, especially since the Chinese government, fearing that inflation in its rapidly growing economy might get out of control, began to put the brakes on in 2014. The Chinese authorities became concerned that the economy was slowing down too fast and themselves implemented QE to prevent 'too hard a landing' in 2015.

Deflation inevitably makes debt problems worse and debts have in fact been increasing. Low interest rates and QE have facilitated the further building up of debt. In July 2014 the Bank for International Settlements reported that debt in the developed economies and in the 'emerging economies', such as China, Brazil, and Turkey, had risen to, in its view, a dangerous level, well beyond where it was before the 2007 crisis. Thus, the very mechanisms used to pull the world out of the post-2007 recession have made the global economy vulnerable to new crises.

Debt and financialization are tied together. Michael Hudson argues that financialization is overwhelming economies with debt, as 'balance-sheet wealth' is created through the lending and borrowing of money rather than productive investment. Thus, to give one example, money is made not so much from building and then selling houses but from lending and borrowing to buy existing houses in the expectation that money can be made from renting them out at a price greater than the interest on the loan or selling them when their price rises. The price bubbles that result may eventually burst with disastrous consequences for borrowers and lenders. Hudson concludes that 'we are passing through a short-lived and unstable phase of "casino capitalism", which now threatens to settle into leaden austerity and debt deflation'.

The spread of industrial production still threatens to produce crises of overproduction, which can only be avoided if consumption can absorb what is produced. The consumption of goods and services in the rich countries of the West is, however, limited by various outcomes of financialization and recession; by the maxing out of household and public debt; by unemployment which remains very high in countries such as Spain; by the lack of income growth amongst wage-earners in countries that are recovering; by the austerity policies of governments.

What about consumption in the rising countries of the East, where economic growth is higher? The Chinese government now gives greater priority to consumption in generating growth. It does seem likely that in the future there will be a big increase in consumption there, and indeed elsewhere in the East. There is, none the less, little sign in 2014 that consumption in China, or for that matter in Japan, which has recently gone into recession, is making up for the weakness of demand in the West. The world economy is still unstably divided between the producer countries of the East and the consumer countries of the West.

The future of capitalism

The weight of these continuing problems might suggest that some final crisis is approaching.

The history of capitalism is, however, littered with crises. Periods of stable economic growth are the exception not the norm. The quarter century of relatively stable economic growth after 1945 may have shaped a generation's expectations about capitalist normality but it was not historically typical of capitalism. Crises are one of its normal features, for there are so many dynamic and cumulative mechanisms operating within it that capitalism cannot be stable for long. The separation of production from consumption, the competition between producers, the conflict between capital and labour, financial mechanisms that inflate and then burst speculative bubbles, the switching of money from one economic activity to another, are all sources of instability that have characterized capitalism from its very beginnings and will no doubt continue to do so.

Particular crises do also eventually come to an end. As the 2007–8 crisis showed, governments can respond quite effectively to crises and their technical capacity to do so has increased as they have learned from experience and developed institutions of intervention. They cannot prevent crises occurring, and they may indeed themselves sometimes generate crises through ill-judged policies and interventions, but they can shorten them when they occur and make them less deep, if they pull the right levers at the right time.

If it is unlikely that capitalism will soon end in some crisis, its current problems do suggest that it may be in a long-term process of decline. This question has been examined in a recent book by Immanuel Wallerstein and others, which considers whether capitalism has a future.

One theme of this book is capitalism's declining capacity to 'externalize' its costs. Capitalist enterprises can only make profits because they pass on the massive environmental, infrastructural, and social costs of their operations to society. These burdens are largely borne by states but their capacity to shoulder them diminishes as governments find themselves forced into expenditure cuts, privatization, and austerity, while a growing inequality, in part resulting from such policies, undermines their legitimacy. Ironically, in pursuit of short term profits private capital uses its considerable power to promote policies that actually weaken the institutions and structures on which capitalism's long term viability rests. According to Craig Calhoun:

> capitalism is destructive of conditions on which capitalism depends—and extreme financialization and neo-liberalism exacerbate this tendency. The future survival of capitalism depends on whether ways can be found to limit or reverse this destruction without eliminating capitalism.

Accumulating problems also result from capitalism's impact on the environment. Here again costs are largely externalized, as in the clearing up of pollution. There is also the problem of the exhaustion of raw materials, for resources are exploited to meet immediate needs and make short-term profits, irrespective of their impact on future availability. Commercial fishing operations are an obvious case in point. There is then the problem of global warming. Private capital commonly fights against policies aimed at reducing the rise of global temperatures, because they increase costs or restrict profitable activities. But, irrespective of their consequences for human lives, the consequences of global warming could eventually bring capitalist economies to a grinding halt at some time in the future.

In which case, 'does capitalism have a future'? In the short term it clearly does. Crises will occur but there is little reason to suppose that one of these will be final. The significance of the longer-term problems outlined above is much more difficult to assess, since the future of capitalism depends not just on capitalism as such but on the way that people respond to its problems. It depends, in other words, on how governments respond, how political and religious movements emerge and develop, how capitalists themselves respond.

Indeed, discussion of the future of capitalism *in general* makes little sense, when there are many different capitalisms to be found around the world. It is the archaic capitalisms of the West, of Europe and the United States, that have been in most trouble. Because these countries have been globally dominant, their problems have been seen as the problems of global capitalism. But, as Michael Mann has pointed out, the recent 'great recession' hardly impacted on South and South-East Asia, and Oceania. The countries in these areas got out of the recession quickly because they had more interventionist states, and because they were less neo-liberal and less financialized than Europe and the United States.

Arguably, the future of capitalism will be shaped not by the institutions and structures of the static or declining countries of the West but the countries of the East. The rising capitalisms of the East are not without problems but they have a dynamism and an institutional distinctiveness that puts them on different trajectories, not only from the West but also from each other. It is important not to lump them together as 'Eastern capitalism'. Japanese, Chinese, and Singaporean capitalism, to name only three prominent variants, do share certain features but they are also very different from each other.

Alternatives?

In considering the future of capitalism, one must also at least briefly consider the alternatives to it. After all, capitalism could come to an end by being overturned by those seeking to install an alternative system.

For a time there was an apparently viable socialist alternative. When the capitalist system was going through the great crisis of the 1930s Depression, an alternative system was under construction in the Soviet Union, which was industrializing on the basis of a non-capitalist, state-socialist economic system. Strong socialist movements in many capitalist industrial societies were still gathering strength and seeking to engineer a shift to such a system. It was not until the decline of labour movements in European societies as the era of marketized capitalism began in the 1980s, and the collapse of the state-socialist economies at the end of that decade that this alternative disappeared.

The opposition to capitalism did not disappear. Anti-capitalist movements continued to exist and have made their presence felt in various ways, notably by organizing large demonstrations to coincide with international economic meetings, as at the 'battle of Seattle' in 1999 and the 'battle of Genoa' in 2001. Although such demos have continued to occur—in June 2013 there was a rather smaller demonstration at Enniskillen against the G8 summit in Ireland—this movement has not maintained its momentum. Indeed, in the book on the future of capitalism, Michael Mann argues that there is no threat to it from the 'global left', which has never been as weak as it is today.

Alternative organizations do exist within capitalist societies. The Mondragon cooperatives in Spain are a well-known example that have been hailed as a working alternative to capitalist organization. Mondragon has been a strikingly successful company that engages in a wide range of economic activities, employs over 80,000 workers, is one of Spain's leading companies, and has numerous subsidiaries in other countries. It operates within the capitalist Spanish economy, however, and it is difficult to see that an organization of this sort can make the leap to organizing a whole economy on a non-capitalist basis. Beneficial as they may be to their members, this is the problem for the alternatives that exist as pockets within capitalist societies.

In the near future at least, it is hard to discern a viable alternative to capitalism. An overthrow of capitalism is unlikely to occur, not only because of the absence of a viable alternative but also because of the immense resources of capitalist corporations and their influence over the state. This does not mean that alternatives have disappeared but the alternatives are not *to* capitalism but *within* capitalism. There are different capitalisms and capitalism has gone through many transformations. Capitalist societies will certainly have to deal with growing problems in the future but their diversity and capacity to change will provide opportunities for reform. Reform does, however, require an engagement with capitalism and cannot be accomplished by movements that stand outside it and merely demonstrate against it.

References

Chapter 1: What is capitalism?

F. Braudel, *The Wheels of Commerce* (William Collins Sons and Co., 1982)

K. N. Chaudhuri, *The English East India Company 1600–1640* (Frank Cass and Co., 1965)

J. Gapper and N. Denton, *All That Glitters: The Fall of Barings* (Hamish Hamilton, 1996)

C. H. Lee, *A Cotton Enterprise 1795–1840: A History of M'Connel and Kennedy* (Manchester University Press, 1972)

H. de Soto, *The Mystery of Capital* (Bantam Press, 2000)

E. P. Thompson, 'Time, Work-discipline, and Industrial Capitalism', *Past and Present*, 38 (1967), pp. 56–97

Chapter 2: Where did capitalism come from?

R. Brenner, 'Agrarian Class Structure and Economic Development in Pre-Industrial Europe', *Past and Present*, 97 (1982), 16–113

C. M. Cipolla, *Before the Industrial Revolution: European Society and Economy 1000–1700*, 3rd edn. (Routledge, 1997)

H. Kamen, *The Iron Century: Social Change in Europe, 1550–1660* (Weidenfeld and Nicolson, 1971)

M. Morishima, *Why has Japan 'Succeeded'?* (Cambridge University Press, 1982)

H. Trevor-Roper, *Religion, the Reformation, and Social Change*, 2nd edn. (Macmillan, 1972)

M. Weber, *The Protestant Ethic and the Spirit of Capitalism* (George Allen and Unwin, 1930)

E. M. Wood, *The Origin of Capitalism: A Longer View* (Verso, 2002)

Chapter 3: How did we get here?

A. Gamble, *The Free Economy and the Strong State: The Politics of Thatcherism*, 2nd edn. (Macmillan, 1994)

S. Arora and A. Charlesworth (Nuffield Trust), E. Kelly and G. Stoye (Institute for Fiscal Studies), *Public Payment and Private Provision* (Nuffield Trust, May 2013)

J. Percy-Smith and P. Hillyard, 'Miners in the Arms of the Law: A Statistical Analysis', *Journal of Law and Society*, 12 (1985), 345–54

A. Pollock, 'How PFI is Crippling the NHS', <www.theguardian.com>, 29 June 2012

D. Yergin and J. Stanislaw, *The Commanding Heights: The Battle for the World Economy* (Simon and Schuster, 1998)

Chapter 4: Is capitalism everywhere the same?

B. E. Aronson, 'Reassessing Japan's "Big Bang": Twenty Years of Financial Regulatory Reform', in C. Gerteis and T. S. George, *Japan since 1945: From Postwar to Post-Bubble* (Bloomsbury, 2013)

A. D. Chandler, *Scale and Scope: The Dynamics of Industrial Capitalism* (Harvard University Press, 1990)

D. Coates, *Models of Capitalism: Growth and Stagnation in the Modern Era* (Polity Press, 2000)

R. P. Dore, *Stock Market Capitalism: Welfare Capitalism: Japan and Germany versus the Anglo-Saxons* (Oxford University Press, 2000)

G. Ingham, *Capitalism* (Polity, 2011)

J. Kingston, *Japan in Transformation 1945–2010*, 2nd edn. (Pearson Education Limited, 2011)

D. Leonhardt and K. Quealy, 'The American Middle Class is No Longer the World's Richest', The Upshot, *New York Times*, 22 April 1914

Organization for Economic Cooperation and Development, *Divided We Stand: Why Inequality Keeps Rising*, 2011 <www.oecd.org/els/social/inequality>

Organization for Economic Cooperation and Development, *Labour*, Statextracts 2014 <http://stats.oecd.org/Index.aspx?DataSetCode=UN_DEN>

T. Piketty, *Capital in the Twenty-First Century* (Harvard University Press, 2013)

D. Pilling, *Bending Adversity: Japan and the Art of Survival* (Allen Lane, 2014)

Y. Sugimoto, *An Introduction to Japanese Society* 3rd. edn. (Cambridge University Press, 2010)

Chapter 5: Has capitalism gone global?

M. Castells, 'Information technology and global capitalism', in *On the Edge: Living with Global Capitalism*, ed. W. Hutton and A. Giddens (Jonathan Cape, 2000)

D. Coates, *Models of Capitalism: Growth and Stagnation in the Modern Era* (Polity Press, 2000)

P. Dicken, *Global Shift: The Internationalization of Economic Activity*, 3rd edn. (Paul Chapman, 1998)

J. Gray, *False Dawn: The Delusions of Global Capitalism* (Granta, 1998)

ONS (Office for National Statistics), *An Examination of Real Wages 2010–2013*, 31 January 2014

T. Piketty, *Capital in the Twenty-First Century* (Harvard University Press, 2013)

A. Sen, 'How to judge globalism', *American Prospect*, 4 January 2002

V. Shiva, 'The World on the Edge', in *On the Edge: Living with Global Capitalism*, ed. W. Hutton and A. Giddens (Jonathan Cape, 2000)

J. Stiglitz, *Globalization and its Discontents* (Allen Lane, 2002)

UNCTAD (United Nations Conference on Trade and Development), *World Investment Report*, 2012

R. Wade, 'Is Globalization Reducing Poverty and Inequality?' *World Development* 32(4), (2004) 567–89

Chapter 6: Crisis? What crisis?

G. Arrighi, *The Long Twentieth Century: Money, Power, and the Origins of Our Times* (Verso, 1994)

E. Hobsbawm, *Age of Extremes: The Short Twentieth Century* (Abacus, 1994)

M. Hudson, <http://michael-hudson.com/2012/08/overview-the-bubble-and-beyond/>

G. Ingham, *Capitalism* (Polity, 2011)

K. Marx and F. Engels, *The Communist Manifesto* ([1848] Penguin, 1967)

R. G. Rajan, *Fault Lines: How Hidden Fractures Still Threaten The World Economy* (Princeton University Press, 2010)

S. Schama, *The Embarrassment of Riches* (Collins, 1987)

I. Wallerstein, R. Collins, M. Mann, G. Derluguian, and C. Calhoun, *Does Capitalism Have A Future?* (Oxford University Press, 2013)

Further reading

Chapter 1: What is capitalism?

Fernand Braudel's three-volume *Civilization and Capitalism: 15th–18th Centuries* (William Collins, 1982–4) is a wonderful source of insight into the nature and early history of capitalism. See especially Volume II, chapters 3 and 4, and the Conclusion to Volume III. On the methods used to discipline and control labour in 19th-century factories, see S. Pollard, *The Genesis of Modern Management* (Penguin, 1968). The excesses of the speculative capitalism of recent years are chronicled by Susan Strange in *Casino Capitalism* (Manchester University Press, 1997) and Michael Hudson in *The Bubble and Beyond: Fictitious Capital, Debt Deflation and the Global Crisis* (Islet, 2012). To read further on Karl Marx, see *Capitalism* (Polity, 2011) by Geoffrey Ingham, which provides an authoritative introduction to the classic theories and basic institutions of capitalism. Hernando de Soto's book, *The Mystery of Capital* (Bantam Press, 2000), contains intriguing reflections, going back to the writings of Adam Smith and Karl Marx, on the character of capitalism and its failure to emerge locally in Third-World countries.

Chapter 2: Where did capitalism come from?

Ellen Meiksins Wood, *The Origin of Capitalism* (Monthly Review Press, 1999) provides a clear and forceful account of the origin of capitalism in Britain and is also the best way into the long-running Marxist debates on this question. In *The Transition from Feudalism to Capitalism* (Macmillan, 1985), R. J. Holton very usefully reviews both

Marxist and non-Marxist theories. There is again much on the origins question in the Braudel volumes listed for Chapter 1. Although it is concerned with broader issues, Volume 1 of Michael Mann's *The Sources of Social Power* (Cambridge University Press, 1986) provides a theory of the origins of capitalism in feudalism and argues that Christianity and the political fragmentation of Europe were also crucial. Mann is much concerned with the distinctiveness of Europe, as is John Hall, who in *Powers and Liberties: The Causes and Consequences of the Rise of the West* (Blackwell, 1985) compares Europe with China, India, and Islamic societies.

Chapter 3: How did we get here?

An influential version of the three-stage approach, though using different labels for the stages, was provided by Scott Lash and John Urry in *The End of Organized Capitalism* (Polity, 1987). The managerial revolution issue is discussed by John Scott, one of the leading researchers in this area, in *Corporate Business and Capitalist Classes* (Oxford University Press, 1997). In *Transformations of Capitalism: Economy, Society and the State in Modern Times* (Macmillan, 2000), Harry F. Dahms has very usefully collected together a number of classic texts on these issues. For a highly readable and globally extensive narrative of the latest transformation, see *The Commanding Heights* by Daniel Yergin and Joseph Stanislaw (Simon and Schuster, 1998). On the privatization of the NHS, see Allyson Pollock *NHS plc: The Privatisation of Our Health Care* (Verso, 2005) and *The End of the NHS: Why the Government Wants to Destroy the Health Service* (Verso, 2015).

Chapter 4: Is capitalism everywhere the same?

Will Hutton's *The State We're In* (Random House, 1994) and John Gray's *False Dawn: The Delusions of Global Capitalism* (Granta, 1998) both argue against the idea that globalization produces convergence, as does David Coates, in *Models of Capitalism: Growth and Stagnation in the Modern Era* (Polity, 2000), which lucidly examines all the major models and claims that each 'has stopped working'. Ronald Dore's *Stock Market Capitalism: Welfare Capitalism* examines the functioning and merits of the German and Japanese models, on the one hand, and those of Britain and America, on the other. While not covering anything like as much ground as the above, my *Labour Movements, Employers, and the State: Conflict and Cooperation in*

Britain and Sweden (Clarendon Press, 1991) uses the notion of suppressed historical alternatives to explore the similarities and differences between Britain and Sweden. In *Bending Adversity: Japan and the Art of Survival* (Allen Lane, 2014), David Pilling provides a brilliant account of recent changes in Japan.

Chapter 5: Has capitalism gone global?

Vandana Shiva's 2000 Reith Lecture, *On Poverty and Globalization*, is available through the BBC's web page. For a comprehensive and clear general account of the development of global capitalism, see Robert Gilpin, *The Challenge of Global Capitalism: The World Economy in the 21st Century* (Princeton University Press, 2000). Susan Strange has chronicled the decisions (and non-decisions) leading to global monetary instability in *Casino Capitalism* (Manchester University Press, 1997). For a World Bank insider's perspective, see Joseph Stiglitz's book, *Globalization and its Discontents* (Allen Lane, 2002). For an outsider's call for fair trade rather than free trade, see George Monbiot's *The Age of Consent: A Manifesto for a New World Order* (Flamingo, 2003).

Chapter 6: Crisis? What crisis?

On tulipomania, see Mike Dash's *Tulipomania* (Indigo, 1999) and Simon Schama's *The Embarrassment of Riches* (Collins, 1987). The best way into Marx's views on capitalism and crisis is to read Part One of *The Communist Manifesto* (originally published in 1848; among other editions, Penguin, 1967). Eric Hobsbawm provides a readable and perceptive account of the Great Depression, the postwar 'golden years', and the 'crisis decades' that followed in his *Age of Extremes* (Abacus, 1994). In his postscript to *Capitalism* (Polity, 2011) Geoffrey Ingham provides a penetrating examination of the 2007 crisis and its aftermath. In *The Bubble and Beyond: Fictitious Capital, Debt Deflation and the Global Crisis* (Islet, 2012), Michael Hudson argues powerfully that a productive capitalism has been succeeded by a financialized and debt-ridden one. Against the background of the crisis, Immanuel Wallerstein, Randall Collins, Michael Mann, Georgi Derluguian, and Craig Calhoun seek boldly to answer the question *Does Capitalism Have a Future?* (Oxford 2013).

Index

Index

Expand your collection of
VERY SHORT INTRODUCTIONS